BEPPE SEVERGNINI

Italian Lessons

Beppe Severgnini is an acclaimed columnist and an editor of Italy's largest-circulation daily newspaper, *Corriere della Sera*. A longtime Italian correspondent for *The Economist* and a frequent contributor to *The New York Times*, he has traveled all over the world. Among his books are the *New York Times* bestseller *La Bella Figura: A Field Guide to the Italian Mind*, *Off the Rails: A Train Trip Through Life*, and the international bestseller *Ciao, America!: An Italian Discovers the U.S.* He lives with his family outside Milan.

ALSO BY BEPPE SEVERGNINI

Ciao, America!: An Italian Discovers the U.S.
La Bella Figura: A Field Guide to the Italian Mind
Off the Rails: A Train Trip Through Life

Italian Lessons

Italian Lessons

Fifty Things We Know About Life Now

BEPPE SEVERGNINI

Translated from the Italian by Antony Shugaar

VINTAGE BOOKS
A Division of Penguin Random House LLC
New York

A VINTAGE BOOKS ORIGINAL, MAY 2022

The Library of Congress has cataloged the Rizzoli edition as follows:
Names: Severgnini, Beppe, author.
Titles: Neoitaliani : un manifesto / Beppe Severgnini.
Description: Prima edizione. | Milan : Rizzoli, settembre 2020.
Identifiers: LCCN 2020472733
Subjects: COVID-19 (Disease)—Italy. |
Italy—Civilization—21st century.
Classification: LCC MLCS 2021/42501 (D)
LC record available at https://lccn.loc.gov/2020472733

Vintage Books Trade Paperback ISBN: 978-0-593-31563-7
eBook ISBN: 978-0-593-31564-4

Author photograph © Daniela Zeda
Photograph on page 185 © Cristopher Porcu
Book design by Steven E. Walker

vintagebooks.com

Printed in the United States of America
1st Printing

In memory of Charlie Conrad, who knew and loved
Italian life and American books

"You put so much stock in *winning* wars," the grubby iniquitous old man scoffed. "The real trick lies in *losing* wars, in knowing which wars can be *lost*. Italy has been losing wars for centuries, and just see how splendidly we've done nonetheless."

—Joseph Heller, *Catch-22*

CONTENTS

There's an Italian Way

Italy arouses in Americans a stunning mix of attraction and skepticism, envy and bafflement, moderate disapproval and incredible allure.

Is there an Italian way of dealing with life? Perhaps there is, and in Italy we're familiar with it. But we're not often willing to talk about it, as if we fear we might reveal a national secret. That's my intention with this book: I want to share that secret with my English-speaking friends and show them the Italian way of doing things.

It may not be the world's best way—is there any such thing as the world's best way?—but it's an interesting way, one that involves adjustment and consolation, tolerance and fantasy. Over the past several decades, it has produced neither impeccable governments nor a roaring economy, if we're honest. But it has displayed elasticity. And in complicated times, elasticity is a great thing. No Italian would be willing to admit what I'm about to say without appending a litany of complaints and grievances, but the fact does remain: we live very nicely in Italy.

The pandemic has scarred the lives of us all in a violent and unpredictable fashion: in the United States, in Europe, and in every country around the world. It has furthermore coincided with other challenges: in the United States it hit at the tail end of Donald Trump's term in office, and in Great Britain it coincided with the implementation of Brexit. In many other countries it marked, isolated, and impoverished society. Each country has reacted in its own fashion. In the Italian reaction, we can discern, one might say, interesting aspects. Actually, useful ones.

Useful to a deeper understanding of who we are in what we used to call the Western world (does that still exist?), what's become of democracy, and how we face up to the great and sweeping changes in individuals and families, relations between parents and children, new gender relations. We Italians aren't new: we have a long history stretching out behind us. Those centuries and millennia of experience don't make us better than anyone else, but perhaps they have given us a few clues that are useful to meeting the challenge of coexistence, keys to that mystery. In this book, I will try to share them with you, my Italy-loving friends. And together we can try to see which doors they can open.

At a time like this, are we happy to be Italians? I think we are. Because I love lists and I detest sermons, I've tried to sum up my convictions in fifty reasons why; fifty reasons for being Italian. I feel certain that not everyone will agree or find these reasons persuasive. I'm sure, in fact, that each of you will have reasons to cut or reasons to add. I'm fine with that. It means thinking together, both writer and readers, in Italy and around the world. That's any author's dream.

These fifty reasons—or lessons, if you prefer—are not a hasty simplification. They constitute the pillars that hold up our very existence, the foundation upon which we have built a significant past and can try to construct a better future. Those pillars have continued to weather storms, even withstanding the Covid-19 tornado, and they have saved us. They include a good national health system; well-tested family relations; functional social structures; the configuration of our cities; underlying generosity, empathy, imagination, and an absence of resignation: Italy has seen far too many things, over its centuries and millennia of history, to raise the white flag in the face of an epidemic. Even the care we lavish on our homes, which may sometimes seem obsessive, has become a welcome and salutary distraction. Our love of cooking—and, why not? our love of wine—has proved to be a blessing. Two good meals a day are a balm for both body and soul.

In all the years of my life and my profession as a journalist, I've traveled the length and breadth of Italy. I've gazed at my country, listened to it, smelled, touched, and tasted it—all of Italy, not just the Lombardy where I was born and raised and still live: every region, every major city, every minor capital of every province, the seas and the mountains, the hills and the lakes, all the islands from my beloved Sardinia to the mysterious Sicily. I've caught Italy doing things I didn't like, I've lost my temper with it frequently, and now and then I've quarreled with it openly. But Italy is my country; I'll never have another. I believe I know its shortcomings and finest qualities. And I'm convinced that our finest qualities far outweigh our shortcomings.

What you're about to read is a book I'd been thinking about for some time. I'd previously tried to sum up Italy and the Italians for the benefit of foreigners as early as 2005. The book I wrote then, *La testa degli italiani*, has been translated into fourteen languages—in the United States, it was titled *La Bella Figura: A Field Guide to the Italian Mind*—but it also served as a mirror for many of my own fellow Italians. The reflection it offered of our national image wasn't always a welcome one; there were those who attacked the author, who was holding the mirror. Most Italian readers, however, seemed to guess at what I was trying to provide: an honest self-portrait and some soul-searching.

Non-Italian readers—and I've met them all over the world— have proved to be every bit as perceptive. They understood that I was offering an honest and affectionate summation (two adjectives, by the way, that are by no means incompatible). I was offering the key—*a* key—to opening the Italian mind, a place capable of infuriating and delighting in the short space of a hundred yards and in just ten minutes' time.

I'd planned to stop there. I had no intention of painting a new Italian self-portrait, I assure you. Then came the virus, and it touched the lives of one and all, practically everyone around the world. And Italy, even though we forget this fact from time to time, is a part of the world. The viral season that we Italians have just lived through changed many things: in our homes, in our families, in our relationships, and in our heads. Other things had already changed over the course of the past few years. *It's time to tell the story of the neo-Italians*, I thought to myself.

Let me make one thing clear: This is not a book about the pandemic. It's a book about Italy and the Italians. But in a very real sense, the pandemic helped: any major crisis becomes a truth machine. Covid and its consequences have done more than reveal who we are. They've made it possible to think about who we could become. We've learned something, both as individuals and as a collective. Certainly, these are lessons we'd rather have learned in some very different fashion. But when life decides to teach us a lesson, it doesn't ask permission.

⇀≈⇀

Who have we become, we Italians? It's going to take time to understand just how uncertainty and challenges have changed our national character. But one change has taken place for certain. We used to think we could solve all our own problems in Italy; now we understand that Italy is part of Europe and the world. We used to think that we were sufficient unto ourselves, we used to mock authority and altruism; but those were the exact qualities that rescued us from our plight. We used to ignore, all too often, both competence and science; and those very things saved us. We blithely confided, in recent years, in the certainty that the superfluous was fundamental. Now we know it's not true.

In the midst of our challenges, though, we've had the good sense—the instinct?—to hold tight to the solid elements of our lives, the foundations of our coexistence. And those good, solid things, as I said, withstood the tornado of this pandemic. That is why it's so important, now more than ever before, to try to understand what it is that we like, what consoles us, makes us proud, and holds us together. We will speak, in this book, about patience, endurance, and wisdom—occasionally involuntary wisdom; about public schools and family doctors, small towns and big cities, craftsmen and scientists, fields and cemeteries, trains and books, parks and shops, old habits and new arrivals, beaches dotted with bright colors and restaurants that welcome us when it's pouring down rain.

Happily, none of that has changed.

The viral tornado has forced us to find resources within ourselves—in our cities and our families, in our heads and our hearts—that we never even knew we possessed (though many people around the world had already acknowledged that we did). Not because we're fools, but because we were distracted and prone to bickering. History teaches that when human societies collapse, it's usually due to distraction, softness, and pettiness. The dictatorship of the superfluous doesn't proclaim martial law, doesn't goose-step through the streets. It wins without fighting, after hollowing us out from within.

A great many things will change in the coming months and years. The risks are unmistakable, but I don't place much credence in the prophecies of authoritarian crackdowns bound up with the current recession and the spreading social malaise. Just look what happened in the United States: the majority of voters opted for common sense (Joe Biden), not recklessness (Donald Trump), and that led to a new beginning. In Italy, we haven't been through any decisive elections, but the news hasn't been much different: we chose a laborious normality over the temptations of illusions and conceit.

So are we fated to go on quarreling, arguing, and protesting in Italy? Most assuredly. Have egotists, cynics, and liars vanished from the landscape? Of course not. When we think back on this incredible period, we shall level accusations against certain innocent individuals and we shall surely absolve any number of deeply guilty parties. That said, on the whole, we'll get better. We'll move forward; we won't slip backward. Decades of meticulous observation of this nation convince me that's the way it'll go. The neo-Italians are ready and able to do new things. We don't know what those will be, we don't know how many, we don't know when.

But what we do know is that it will all depend on us.

Fifty Reasons for Being Italian

1. Because when everyone expects us to lose our cool, we find our strength

Italy was the first country outside Asia to experience Covid. It was the first country to order a lockdown, on March 9, 2020. The picture of Italian Army trucks transporting dead bodies in Bergamo is etched into our collective memory. The northern provinces of Brescia, Lodi, and Cremona also suffered deeply: local newspapers were printed cemeteries overflowing with death notices, and every single day another acquaintance or friend died. Crema, where I was born and still live, was a ghost town for two months. People were in a state of anguish. But they stayed home.

In May 2020, Italy cautiously reopened. Limited exercise and athletic activity was allowed, outdoors, and then came visits to one's family, partners, and lovers ("stable affections" was the government's terminology, which triggered a national debate on what made affections stable rather than otherwise). Factories and construction firms went back to work. A few days later, amid jockeying and corner cutting, so did shops, cafés, and restaurants. Schools remained closed, for who knows what reason. Masking remained obligatory. We all wore light blue reminders on our faces of what had happened, of what must not happen again.

Italy went through a process that was reproduced, over varying time lines, in every country hit by the virus: first underestimating the danger; then disbelief, anxiety, and lockdown. Then the reactions: wisecracks and memes on our smartphones, mood swings, the reassurance of the national anthem. By then we had understood. The fight was going to be a long-distance race; so we started running.

In Crema, the hospital was overwhelmed by patients, many of them in critical condition, in desperate need of intensive care. The Italian Army built a field hospital in the parking lot in just a few days. A fifty-two-member medical brigade, made up of doctors and nurses, arrived from Cuba to help us. For the entire month of April, ambulance sirens filled the air. All around were blue skies, flowering trees, and the most beautiful springtime in many years.

Now that all these things have become memories, we can finally say it: we survived. I described some of these things in the *New York Times*. The headline was "How Italy Coped, and Will Keep Coping." We finally had confirmation of that fact—after a criminally distracted summer—in fall and winter, before the national vaccination campaign. It wasn't just a battle; it was a full-blown war, filled with anxiety and grief and resulting in more than five million cases and 140,000 deaths, though the numbers are probably much higher. Sixty million people, all told, did follow the rules—surprisingly, considering our reputation for lack of self-discipline.

But is it really so surprising?

In Italy, we don't respect—or ignore—rules the way people do elsewhere. We take it as an insult to our intelligence to be expected to follow a regulation without first having thoroughly argued the fine points; any regulation at all, be it legal, moral, social, or tax or traffic related. Blind obedience is considered beneath us. We want to make up our minds about whether a given rule should apply to our specific case. Once we've come to the conclusion that it does apply, we obey it. Faced with the threat of the virus, we decided that the lockdown made good sense, and we complied. It wasn't a collective decision. It was the cumulative result of millions of individual decisions.

We succeeded in part because we had the social and psychological resources to do so: realism, resilience, inventiveness, the support of extended families, an instinct for altruism and generosity—at times bordering on the exhibitionistic.

We were aided by the fact that we are a sociable people. The internet provided new tools that came in handy during the emergency. Personal and family ties—the importance of which has produced a great deal of second-rate writing and opining around the world but that nonetheless should not be underestimated—proved crucial. Men cooked, cleaned house, and tidied their rooms as they'd never done before. If they had children, they spent more time with them. Every mother turned into a schoolteacher, adding that task to all her others. Friends pitched in and helped one another out. Aperitifs on Zoom or on balconies didn't go on for long. But the strength and the patience that we displayed, after we put down our drinks, were surprising.

A pandemic—like a war, like any serious crisis—tells you a lot about both yourself and others. It helps us to better understand people, communities, organizations, and nations.

The United States of America sprang out of a popular rebellion, and the cult of individual freedom persists in the national culture, as we have seen. From Michigan to Pennsylvania, citizens in great numbers—some of them armed—took to the streets to demand a rapid reopening, egged on by the president himself—none other than Donald Trump—who initially minimized the risks and then proceeded to order the restrictions. The shock waves unleashed by Covid—social, economic, and political—led to the Black Lives Matter movement and subsequently to the electoral overthrow of Trump himself.

France has always shown a certain gift for protest marches in the street, and sure enough, protest marches there have been: first on the outskirts of Paris and then in the heart of the city, featuring doctors and nurses among others. The Swedes believe in an open society, and theirs was one of the final countries to order a lockdown, and even then only reluctantly. The Russians are resigned to strong state power, and they experienced it once again with Covid: no one knows exactly what happened. In Great Britain, minimizing is a semiofficial state religion; this time, however, British understatement was a factor in the government's underestimation of the threat. Only the personal drama of Prime Minister Boris Johnson—admitted to the hospital on an emergency basis and coming dangerously close to death—persuaded the British to revise their point of view. Not everyone, of course: conspiracy theorists and political amateurs—just coming off the years of Brexit—expanded their fanciful interpretations to the spreading epidemic. In time, though, Great Britain got itself organized—once again in keeping with British tradition.

In Italy, there was no fighting in the streets, few if any protest marches, no violence, and certainly no sign of an armed revolt. Here and there you heard, at most, understandable mutterings of discontent at the dithering and hesitation of various administrations in the regional and the national governments. The beginning of the vaccination campaign was chaotic and featured episodes of highly contagious selfishness. But the vast majority of Italians—north, south, in all walks of life, and no matter the level of educational achievement—made up their minds that the lockdown made sense; reluctantly but reliably, they therefore stopped going out and avoided gathering with others. For once, the government owes the governed a sincere and wholehearted thank-you.

Italians have given ample proof that they are capable of being patient and, if necessary, even diligent. What we need now is better organization, greater rapidity, and higher precision. But we live in emotional times, and feelings are the fuel that runs Italy. They can drive the nation forward toward a better future, or they can make it stumble at the (re-)starting line. That's the eternal dilemma we face. Only this time, we're risking much, much more.

2. Because we're vulnerable when we think we're tough, and vice versa

Many things have changed since that long-ago spring of 2020—not just the government in office. We've all changed in Italy. The reaction to the emergency required empathy, decisiveness, and a capacity for imagination: all qualities that are specialties of the house (or perhaps we should say *della casa*). Today we need calm and foresight.

The impression is that the burst of emotional saccharine has wearied many if not most. But we thrive on relations, interactions, personal exchanges. Virtual encounters have become popular in Italy, as everywhere, but they tend to leave us unsatisfied. Depriving the Italians of their emotions is like stripping the Swiss of their predictability: it's traumatic.

The pandemic taught us one lesson: in Italy, we're no longer accustomed to uncertainty. We are psychologically fragile. There's no need to be ashamed, no reason to be surprised. We're citizens of the Granted States of Fulfilled Western Wishes. The risks of everyday life in other parts of the world—health risks; food risks; climate, political, police, and military risks—are unknown to those who live in Italy and Europe. It would be interesting to know what young Africans think of Covid after facing the challenges and dangers of the desert, Libyan prisons, and the Mediterranean crossing: they might surprise us.

Over the centuries, epidemics have been greeted by rumor mills and word of mouth, a network that can turn into mob frenzy and poisonous slander (Alessandro Manzoni famously described the process in *The Betrothed*). Nowadays, we know a great deal, and we learn it very quickly: probably too quickly. We're hyperinformed and hypersensitive. We've just been through the first social media pandemic: the news reports we exchanged—by voice, text, and picture—were fraught with emotion and highly fragmented. The overabundance of information—as often as not imprecise and occasionally downright false—became a feeder of anxiety. Virologists and epidemiologists, frequently quite talkative, deserve a share of the blame: captivated by the spotlight, some of them only contributed to the confusion.

Why have we become so sensitive? Perhaps because, along with the decline in risk, there has been a corresponding drop in the unexpected. As we go about our days, we carry a device in our pockets that allows us to know traffic conditions, the location of the car on its way to pick us up, the weather report, the distance left to travel. There is still the occasional unpredictable turn of events, as we know; but we've corralled them into a special holding pen, as in the game of Monopoly.

The tools and devices at our disposal have made us unaccustomed to the sort of unpredictability that was an everyday reality to previous generations. Perhaps that is why we so fear diseases, which have marked the extent of human history. The fact that we've conquered so many is wonderful; but it leaves us psychologically vulnerable in the face of those that persist. Hypochondria has stopped being a pathological condition; instead it's become a feature of the Italian condition.

There's a family story that I'll never forget. My father, Angelo, was born in 1917 in a farmhouse in Offanengo, in the Crema countryside, the seventh child in a farming family. He caught the Spanish flu, which between 1918 and 1920 killed between fifty and a hundred million people around the world and six hundred thousand in Italy. His parents left him in a cradle in an underheated room, confiding in providence: they had other children to worry about. My father recovered and survived: for nearly a hundred years. He often told us that story, the details of which were confirmed by my aunts, who at the time were in their teens. It was a fact of life: a century ago, it wasn't rare for a large family to lose a daughter or a son.

They were cruel times, which nobody wants to see return; times that spread a patina of fatalism across the population at large, a patina that verged on resignation, on the one hand, and raw courage, on the other. Today we are stronger and, at the same time, weaker. Medicine has made giant strides. The public health system, along with free, mandatory education, is our society's greatest achievement. But we struggle to accept that there are still phenomena that are difficult to control, events that force us to use ancient words: *contagion, quarantine, isolation.*

I wonder if we'll actually learn anything from what has happened and is still happening—for instance, whether we'll remember how fragile we are and how badly we need the help of others; whether we'll understand that as we pass through this world, we can confront difficulties better by joining forces and uniting our understanding. In the face of the virus and everything else.

3. Because we can be serious about things, but we hate to admit it

Expressing our thanks was a required gesture of appreciation: thanking, seeing, and greeting them without wasting their valuable time. Because anyone who's pitching a field hospital in just three days is too busy to indulge in idle conversation. When I arrived there, I leaned my bike on its kickstand: in all, I had pedaled seven hundred meters from my home. I'd never dreamed I'd see cranes, trucks, and yellow tents marked with red crosses in the parking lot in front of the emergency room, right behind the shuttered newsstand. Crema is a small city, brisk, no-nonsense, and strong. But Crema needed outside help in March 2020, and that help was forthcoming. The central hospital, Ospedale Maggiore—which at first was the one providing assistance to Codogno and the surrounding Bassa Lodigiana plain—could no longer fend for itself.

The Third Medical came riding to its rescue. Based in Bellinzago Novarese, the Italian Army platoon-sized medical unit consisted of thirty men. Lieutenant Colonel Michele Ricci, who commanded the unit, explained to me that fifteen of them would be deployed in Crema even after the field hospital had been set up: thirty-two patients were under care, three of them in intensive care. Then a Cuban medical brigade arrived and was given lodging at the local diocese's Caritas facilities. The Milano unit medical staff were housed in the former courthouse. Local businesses, ranging from tow trucks to plumbing and electrical contractors and cleaning services, all refused payment for their work. On Sunday, March 28, the military's

work was done. On the following Monday, Crema's doctors
and health care professionals began working in coordination
with their Cuban colleagues. On Tuesday, the first patient was
admitted to the field hospital. After that, patients came pouring in, an unbroken flood, at all hours of the day and night, for
the following month.

Michele Ricci is originally from Massafra in Taranto province, the instep of the Italian "boot," and he's been deployed on
missions to Kosovo, Afghanistan, and Iraq. Seeing him arrive
in Crema had something of the surreal about it. The ambu-
lances just wouldn't stop coming: it was the same sound as
always, but we weren't the same as before. We walked through
the rapidly rising field hospital facilities with Crema's mayor,
Stefania Bonaldi. She was exhausted, but she still managed
to put a smile on her face, albeit behind her mask. She and I
have been acquainted for years. In Crema, everybody knows
everybody else. We knew the dead, we knew those who were
sick but still in their homes. Some were doctors, close friends
of ours. All around us was the delicate sunlight of early spring.
It seemed almost to be mocking us.

I returned home and wrote to the commander of the unit,
Lieutenant Colonel Ricci, thanking him. He wrote back almost
instantly, expressing surprise: *Of course. This is our home,
isn't it?*

Forty years ago, when I was writing for the Cremona newspaper *La Provincia* as a way to take my mind off my legal studies, I had a weekly column called "Parlar sul Serio": "Speaking
Seriously." It was a fairly obvious pun—Serio is the name of
the river that runs through my hometown, Crema—but it was

also a fairly *accurate* pun. We're very serious around these parts, the way that Italians know how to be serious. But we hate to admit it.

We've cultivated a reputation as being brilliant but unreliable. Reliability, in Italy, is an unconscious quality—one of the many such qualities in a country that fears praise, as if it were somehow likely to ruin our reputation. We know how to be serious, but we're reluctant to admit it. Then the days of viruses and fear come upon us, and we suddenly realize that we're different; suddenly solid, cohesive, and capable of meeting the challenge.

Try telling other people this. They'll reply that we Italians have remained a band of individualists, fatalistic and self-centered. There certainly are people like that in Italy, and they can be found in large numbers. The majority, in fact, respond to challenges by lodging complaints, leveling accusations, insinuating suspicions, and detailing how they've been inconvenienced. But they respond. Too much has happened in this ancient and elongated nation. If we'd been incapable of reacting, Italy would no longer exist, and even the notion of Italy would now be a long-forgotten idea. There's a trace amount of optimism, in our national personality, and we're secretly proud of the fact. *Infidum hominem malo suo esse cordatum,* "The man who is incapable of illusion may be sensible but only to his detriment," Saint Augustine wrote. It's clear that we were already that way even then.

I'm not one of those people who love their own homeland and detest the homelands of others. I'm born of Crema, Cremona, with a smidgen of Bergamo in my blood, Milanese by adoption and out of gratitude, Lombard by family, Italian in my heart, a European by conviction, with deep ties to the United States, and an impassioned student of the world. That doesn't mean I don't know how to choose. In fact, I've chosen very well. Except for one thing: I didn't choose the place of my birth. But the people who chose that for me, I have to say, did an excellent job.

There are times, I'll admit, when I take for granted the prosperity and harmony that surround me. But then someone or something will come along and help me to appreciate them. The light on the roofs from my terrace, the aerial acrobatics of the swallows. The family photographs that, during our lockdown, popped out of their wooden boxes. An unexpected guest who lets me see through his eyes. A film such as *Call Me by Your Name*, in which Crema and its surrounding countryside became luminous protagonists. The memory of so many nighttime rambles with my friends, back when we were just kids; each of us insisted on walking the others home, just to make sure we'd never have to stop talking. Or else the threat you can't see coming: a virus that devastates your proud little city, suddenly filling the hospital to bursting and emptying the piazzas, and then proceeds to torture us for more than a year, forcing us to think about what's important and what isn't. And persuading us that we're stronger together. We've come to that realization, in Crema and all over Italy.

But of course, we don't want to admit it.

4. Because we're unpredictable, but not unreliable

Two adjectives are frequently applied to us Italians: *sociable* and *undisciplined*. In fact, during the Covid pandemic, we've shown the world that we know how to be disciplined, and we've willingly sacrificed the time we'd normally spend with others. Suddenly we've stopped being afraid of things, places, words, and situations, and we've started fearing other people: bodies, contact, even breathing. It's a new instinct that has left us uncomfortable. We belong to a sensual culture. But we possess realism, resilience, and social networks. During the most stark and dramatic moments of our recent history—the world wars, the civil war, domestic and international terrorism—we've discovered surprising resources.

Years ago, during a book tour I did in the United States, someone asked me to sum up Italy in a brief description. I replied, "Neither heaven nor hell. A charming purgatory full of restless souls, each one convinced they're special." And, in fact, those very same souls have shown that special individuals, in extraordinary times, save themselves by doing eminently normal things; for example, by respecting the rules.

Many people, as I have written, doubted that we'd be able to do it. Prejudices die hard. There is a systematic suspicion concerning our intrinsic unreliability as Italians. In an interview with National Public Radio (NPR), at the start of Italy's first lockdown, I didn't hold back: instead of doubting that we Italians will be able to get this done, I asked, why don't you Americans start getting organized? Among other things, in the United States you don't have a national health service, where everyone can be given proper care, without questions first and without bills for service afterward.

What about the cynics who rushed out all over the country to stroll through narrow lanes in multitudes in spite of the prohibitions? What about the Italians who gathered en masse with the excuse of politics (Rome), soccer (Milan, Naples), aerobatics (Turin), discotheques (Sardinia), and beaches (Liguria, Veneto, Lazio, Sicily)?

They, too, were Italians, of course. Reckless Italians. Italians confused, first of all, by the sudden firmness of their government's position and bewildered by the contradictory instructions issued and then exhausted and anxious and eager for some distraction. These aren't justifications, but they are explanations, and they help us understand.

The Pollyannas and the Chicken Littles in our midst have put the rest of us onto a head-spinning emotional roller coaster. No doubt they'll do it again. Public health and vaccines. Work, nuclear families, and travel. Schools and sports. Incomes and reparations. We veer continually from optimism to pessimism, buffaloed by a photograph, a prediction, a statistic, or a text message. We needn't be ashamed, but we do need to climb down off the emotional seesaw now that the emergency is over. It's inevitable at times: anyone can be anxious and unpredictable. But right now, we must prove that we know how to be calm and reliable.

Were we afraid when the epidemic was spreading? What if we were? Sometimes fear is just a form of wisdom. Recklessness is almost always a mark of immaturity. If we managed not to lose our heads entirely, if we were able to demonstrate some self-confidence, if we faced up to the world's skepticism and refuted it with our actions, then we can now safely say: We are Italians. Never underestimate us.

5. Because we make gallant gestures. Good behavior? We're still working on that.

If I were asked to identify the foremost weakness of our national character, I'd have to say this: We Italians place too much emphasis on hunches and improvisation, of which we are past masters, and too little on thorough preparation. We are so attracted by what is beautiful that we sometimes prefer it to what is good. And that's partly because achieving what is good—let's admit it—is hard work. In Italian, and only in Italian, is there an expression such as *la bella figura*. Just think: it's an aesthetic consideration. *Bella figura*: we want to cut a fine figure, not make a good impression.

Fine gestures meet that need, and we've seen that in our own recent and challenging past. There's a theatrical aspect to Italian generosity, though that in no way undercuts its sincerity. If anything, it simply makes it more spectacular. Ours is a sophisticated exhibitionism. We have no real need of witnesses or onlookers; we are psychologically sufficient unto ourselves. We are at once actor and audience: we give ourselves our own standing ovations, silently, every time we perform a good deed. So what's the underlying problem? It's that we love fine gestures to such a degree that we prefer them to simple good behavior. But ten good deeds don't make a man good, any more than ten sins transform him into a sinner. Theologians distinguish between *actum* and *habitus*: the single episode counts much less than does the habitual action.

Basically, are you interested in understanding Italy? Put aside your guidebooks. Study theology.

During the pandemic, I frequently wondered: What will we do after this? How will we act? Will we remember the discipline we proved capable of, a discipline that allowed us to ward off far more serious consequences?

The fact that the emergency has been overcome—and that the tragedy did not proliferate into catastrophe—was also in part to our credit. Some of us more than others, of course. Loan sharks and con artists never sleep, and here, too, they were out in force. But how many of them were there? Instead, let's think of the hospital workers, and the risks they ran; the millions of fellow Italians who got up and went to their jobs with heavy hearts day after day, for more than a year.

There is a man who helped Italy feel good about itself. His name is Francesco Paolo Figliuolo. He is a general of the Alpini, the mountain corps—unusual for someone born in tiny Basilicata, which lies in the heel of Italy's boot, very far from the Alps. He was the head of the Logistics Command of the Italian Army when, in March 2021, Prime Minister Mario Draghi appointed him extraordinary commissioner for the Covid emergency. His task was to sort out the lagging vaccination campaign and to rein in Italy's twenty regions, each of which tended to act on its own.

General Figliuolo started to tour the country in his uniform, with the Alpini's distinctive feather in his hat and a plateau of decorations on his chest—he had led an Italian force in Afghanistan and the international mission in Kosovo and was proud of them. Uniforms are not often seen in Italy, and there were complaints ("It's inappropiate," said Vincenzo De Luca, the governor of Campania). General Figliuolo shrugged. In a few weeks he mounted a vast, lean, and effective vaccination campaign, which everyone praised. His favorite line in private was "I'm an Alpino, but I'm not stupid."

We've been a surprise, we Italians, even to ourselves. Will we succeed in surprising ourselves even more—and surprising the rest of Europe—or will we go back to our old characteristics of self-interest and self-absolution? If that happens, it would be a grave case of backsliding—one we cannot afford.

6. Because the rest of the world looks at you; Italians see you

Demanding challenges—as we've said—reveal the true substance of people, societies, and nations. You can pretend for a day, a week, or a month; after that, it becomes impossible. This is true of both representatives and those represented, those who govern and those who are governed, administrators and the administered. It's true of public figures. It's true of all us Italians as we struggle with the most overwhelming challenge of this century.

Have you ever read *The Shadow-Line*? It's a very famous book, but very famous books tend to have one disadvantage: they're taken for granted, treated as if already read. Some of them, though, really deserve to be read. This novella by Joseph Conrad, for instance. Written in 1915 and published in 1917, it was one of his final works. It's a confession, as stated in the full original title (*The Shadow-Line: A Confession*). The young protagonist—never called by any name—takes command of a ship, his first command, and finds himself motionless on a still sea, the crew prostrate under the blows of fever and fear. But he toughs it out, completes the voyage, and realizes that he has crossed the shadow line that separates youth from maturity. He's become an adult.

We aren't aboard the vessel *Orient*, sailing from Bangkok to Singapore. The ordeal to which the pandemic subjected us was nevertheless grueling. We would gladly have avoided it if we could have. But perhaps it helped us to become a little more grown-up. To look inside of ourselves. And to see those around us.

We're good at this, we Italians. Out of generosity, out of curiosity, out of sheer self-interest; but we do know how to see people, we don't stop at just looking at them. "People" is a concept that thrills professional politicians, because it allows them to flatter everyone; in daily life, wisely, we use the term sparingly; it's too generic, too predictable. In Italy, as anywhere else, there are good people and bad people, generous people and selfish people, agreeable people and annoying people. You have to know how to tell them apart.

There was no need for a pandemic to convince me of the Italian capacity for observation, which blends curiosity, altruism, impatience, and an inability to mind one's own business. I remember where I was when I heard the concept expressed for the first time, with conviction and clarity: the Italians don't just look at you; the Italians *see* you.

At the University of St. Andrews in eastern Scotland, about fifteen years ago, I was doing a book presentation, an event that was open to the public. When I finished my little talk, we moved on to the ritual of questions for the author. A young woman stood up; she might have been twenty-five. She was very attractive: blonde, athletic, with a smile on her face and a direct, open glance. She said, without any preamble, "I'm going to marry an Italian." I thought she must be joking, so I replied, in the same spirit, "I see no problem with that, signorina. You have many millions to choose from. You may wish to inform his wife, if that seems necessary." She overlooked my sexist answer—unthinkable nowadays, especially at a university!—and continued undeterred, "Do you want to know why I'm going to marry an Italian? Because before living in Italy, I lived in South Africa, Israel, and Germany, and now

I'm here, in Great Britain. In all of these places, people look at you. But only in Italy do they *see* you."

That was when I realized what she was trying to tell me. The Italian ability to see people is a real thing. And it's not limited to young women, as movies and lesser literature would have one believe. We Italians are too restless and too filled with empathy to ever overlook the possibilities offered by an encounter with another human being. Whether because we're face-to-face with a tall person or a short person, a young person or a not-so-young person, a person with a great deal of hair or far too little, a person wearing a strange scarf or with a pleasant voice—whether on account of a shirt or a hairstyle, a smile or an adjective: any excuse is perfectly valid, in Italy, to pay attention to a fellow human being.

You can glimpse it in many different situations. In the interactions between a police officer and a citizen, between a conductor and a passenger on a train, between a shopkeeper and a customer: every time, it's unmistakable that no one is a number, we're all onstage, we're all part of the play. The gaze isn't necessarily benevolent. But it's a little more extended, and silence is rare. If life is a performance, we're interested in all the actors, both the stars and the uncredited extras.

In the rest of the world, they look at you; in Italy, they *see* you.

7. Because we find unexpected heroes

The phones and computers of many residents of Crema stuck at home in the lockdown lit up with photographs and recollections: Francesco waving his oversized hands; Francesco bursting into his grand baritone laugh; Francesco riding away on his bicycle after forgiving us. Covid carried him off in April 2020. Francesco Valcarenghi, born in 1936, the *bidello*, or custodian and hall monitor at the Liceo Classico Racchetti, the humanities high school of Crema, between 1970 and the mid-1990s. A *bidello-insegnante*, or custodian and teacher in the etymological sense of the word: someone who left a *segno*, someone who left a mark.

If he were on staff today, Francesco would be a member of Psychological Support Outside the Classroom, or PSOC (an acronym that might well be adopted eventually by the Italian Ministry of Education). We learned a great deal from him. We received very little civic education in the classroom but a great deal in the hallway. The halls were Valcarenghi's domain, and his world revolved around three fixed points: the Torino FC soccer team, the Italian Socialist Party (Partito Socialista Italiano, or PSI), and *Il Giorno*, the newspaper from which he drew all his topics of discussion and argumentation. Among his most frequent adversaries were Juventus FC and Italy's Christian Democratic Party, two entities that aroused a certain feeling of mistrust in him, for reasons that were not all that different.

He was proud of his professional title, *il bidello Francesco*.

If any of us had ever referred to him as "auxiliary personnel," he'd have lifted us off the ground by our clavicles with those hands of his, trained, as a very young man, in a butcher shop; we certainly wouldn't have done it twice. I remember him in the mornings at the front door. He filled it all, tall and power- fully built as he was, his arms crossed: he greeted latecomers with a glare and a wry observation. Just think of Clint East- wood in *The Good, the Bad and the Ugly.* He was the Good, we were the Small and, by and large, the Ugly; but there was no one in the school who could be branded the Bad.

Not even the teaching staff. A few of our teachers were excellent; the others were good or at least up to snuff. Every so often one of them would try to become an authoritarian, with modest results (between 1970 and 1975, teaching was more or less like trying to herd cats). Francesco was no authoritarian; he was authoritative. He'd earned our respect by explaining what was right and what was wrong, according to his lights. He never insisted that we agree with him. But he did want us to make an effort to be able to identify that distinction: right, on the one hand; wrong, on the other. The rest, he would say, can come later.

Leave something behind you: a wake, a trace, a mark, a good memory. Everyone aspires to do that, a sanctioned rebellion against the spectacular absurdity of life. Luca Nicolini leaves more behind him than just affection and esteem: he also leaves the Mantua Literary Festival, known as *festivaletteratura*. He founded it in 1997 with his wife, Carla Bernini, and a group of friends. What it grew into, you probably know: the finest literary festival in all of Europe. And not just according to us

Italians; British, American, African, Asian, Israeli, and Arab writers all agree. It's a movable feast, where writers meet readers, pages become voices, and everyone present learns something new.

I've been attending the festival since 1998. On the occasion of the twentieth edition of the festival, in 2016, I suggested an event dedicated to the great writers who passed through Mantua, those who are no longer among us. A young colleague on the *Corriere della Sera*, Stefania Chiale, helped me out. We called it "To Absent Friends." Great names of literature, authors Italian and not, celebrated names and others less well known: we summoned them all on Piazza Castello through archival video and audio, books, and readings. I'd never have imagined that soon enough, Luca would be another of those absent friends.

He was a person of sterling character. He had fine taste, he was generous, and he fostered fierce antipathies. He was able to withstand the pressures and temptations of politics. But he was also admirable in his ability to resist the giantism, the unbridled growth, that menaces any successful initiative, not only those in the field of culture. The *festivaletteratura* remained on a scale compatible with the size of Mantua, and Mantua is no metropolis. It's a perfect set for the film of words, with tens of thousands of actors and no screenplay.

Luca called me on April 25, 2020, in the afternoon. It was a blue springtime Saturday. I was out in my garden, and the linden and mulberry trees and the rosebushes were smiling at Italy's fear. His voice came across clear and calm. He already knew how his story would end, but he had an idea for afterward, and he wanted to talk to me about it. He also knew that the *festivaletteratura* is in excellent hands and no danger. The Mantuans know it, too, and they've filled the city's windows and balconies with their blue volunteer T-shirts.

Only those we are in the process of forgetting really die. The world of books will surely remember my friend Luca Nicolini.

The Cuban medical brigade departed with people clapping and cheering, with the May sunlight that reflected joyously off the broad forehead of the regional commissioner, with the bells of Crema Cathedral pealing full tilt, preventing the Cuban ambassador from finishing his address. He turned to the bishop and asked, "How long will this go on?" The bishop replied seraphically, "Another minute or two."

That marked the end of my long return home, a way of sharing my grieving hometown's uncertainty. Our mayor, Stefania Bonaldi, said, "Battles aren't won by solitary heroes, they're won by communities. We have been a people, not a crowd driven by fear." And she's right. She did her job well, our team leader, who loves running and Facebook; and so did the other mayors of the Crema area. She is a member of the leftist Italian Democratic Party; the others for the most part fall on the right of the political spectrum. They worked together from the very outset, doing what politics in Lombardy no longer seems to know how to do.

Crema was strong because it remained united. When forced to choose between complaining and rolling up its shirtsleeves and working together, the city had no doubts. We all knew one another on the Venetian piazza, and the authorities seemed to realize that fact. They stayed out of the way.

The fifty Cuban doctors and nurses who came to support our struggling hospital wore red T-shirts bearing the name of their country: CUBA. They seemed festive: mission accomplished, time to return home, loaded down with gifts and gratitude. For the gifts they were obliged to pay a supplemental baggage fee on the flight back. The gratitude, on the other hand, traveled free of charge.

The worst of the *pandemia de la Covíd*, as the Cuban ambassador, José Carlos Rodríguez Ruiz, called it, had passed. Under a blue sky, as the Henry Reeve Brigade left with its medals, what remained behind were the people of Crema, tired now, with their memories and their sense of relief. The geriatrician Fabio Bombelli remained, seated on a bench beneath the portico. We've known each other since we were children, and he played a mean game of basketball. Of all my doctor friends who've contracted Covid—seven out of ten—he was the one who had it worst. "The important thing is to be here to tell the story," he said, smiling from behind his mask. He'd already gone back to work. Crema is in Italy, and that—with a few exceptions—is the way Italy works.

8. Because we do learn, one way or another

As I looked at pictures of the people fleeing Milan on the evening of Saturday, March 7, 2020, just prior to the announcement of the first Lombard lockdown (also the first Italian lockdown, the first European lockdown), I was reminded of a short story by Dino Buzzati. It's titled "Qualcosa era successo" ("Something Had Happened") in Italian, though it was published as "Catastrophe" in English. The main character is returning to Milan by train, and he realizes that outside everyone is going in the opposite direction: they're running away by any means available. He leans out the window and shouts a question. Everyone is running; no one replies. He reaches out to grab a newspaper in a station; he's left with nothing but a triangular scrap of the front page, with the last letters of a banner headline: . . . TION. Everyone is fleeing something that ends in *-tion*. Revolution? Conflagration? Military occupation? Insurrection? He can't say. The train is rushing toward this thing, whatever it is.

Infection, too, ends in *-tion*. In the face of Covid's onslaught, more than a few people were tempted to drop everything and flee. Panic, like the virus itself, is cunning: it knows how to worm its way into our minds and our hearts. Nearly the entire population of Milan, Buzzati's fellow citizens, resisted the urge to run away, however. The city held out, as did the rest of Italy: even the parts of Italy not haunted by the sound of ambulance sirens to remind everyone of what was happening—and sadly, what *had* happened.

We've learned so many things: the people we care about, the people who care about us; the generosity of many and the frightened selfishness of a few; the importance of certain professions, which far too many of us take for granted. Doctors and nurses, obviously, but also so many others who keep Italy running. Let us think of all those who work—who still work— the cash registers of the supermarkets; let's thank them, at least. Why not? It's something we can still do.

We learned the meaning of our home space, the difference between what is necessary and what is superfluous, the consolation of corners and objects that we'd long ago forgotten how to see. I'm certain that we all looked at photographs, records, and books with new, appreciative eyes.

We learned that forced cohabitation can test our relationships, for better or worse (just ask anyone who's spent their vacations in a tent, in a camper, or on a boat!). But we've also realized that distance is a scale; it allows us to gauge the weight of certain relationships. The social minuet to which we'd grown accustomed suddenly struck us as grotesque. I confess that I've gained a renewed appreciation for certain friendships in the recent past. Others have left me baffled, in some cases even disappointed. I've forgotten still others, and they've forgotten me. I feel sure the same has happened to you.

We've learned the revolutionary beauty of the internet and social media, if used properly; the importance of good company, because the pandemic was especially tough on those who live alone, both in Italy and abroad. Let's not forget the young Italians scattered across Europe and around the world. Few of them were able to return home before lockdown; many countries limited or prevented their attempts to travel.

We've even rediscovered the balcony, where we had stopped leaning out or, when we did, doing so only absentmindedly.

The return of old Italian classics: balconies, terraces, loggias, verandas, and sundecks have for centuries played starring roles in our operas, stories, and dramas, from *Romeo and Juliet* to Benito Mussolini's speeches. The music, the salutations, and the *aperitivi* enjoyed in the company of others were not just an excuse for a photo on Instagram. It didn't last long, predictably. But it was proof that we're more closely united than we think—and that when the going gets tough, we draw on resources none of us suspected were there.

And that we do learn, one way or another.

9. Because we've seen practically everything; the rest we imagine

All peoples, and naturally the individuals who make up those peoples, obey neither the dictates of their own best interests, much less the pure dictates of reason; instead, they are dominated by imagination. Everything we do, we do it because imagination demands it. La folle du logis, *the madwoman of the house: that is the explanation of why history, which would be appalling if it were rational and mechanical if it were economic in nature, is as unpredictable, illogical, and attractive as any novel.*

That opinion dates from 1958 and was expressed by Giuseppe Prezzolini, one of the most astute scholars of the Italian character. The Italian imagination is not the madwoman of the house, a form of inevitable folly. It is, rather, the guide to which everyone in Italy, sooner or later, pays attention. Imagination combined with passion: together they're capable of both masterpieces and disasters, often in rapid succession.

We Italians have an idea of the country we'd like to live in, and it might serve as a useful lesson for the rest of the world. We're in search of a harmony of which we catch just glimpses of on certain evenings, in certain piazzas, on a terrace or in a train station in the morning, at those moments when all of Italy seems to breathe together, without the slightest idea of how it's managed to do it.

That happened during the lockdown, undoubtedly. It can happen again. Not always: that would be illogical and unnatural. But we needn't be afraid of the society that we imagine—

more just, a little cleaner, more united—because it's within our reach. What's holding us back is cynicism, a form of self-defense that in Rome, as we shall see, has been elevated to a full-fledged martial art. There's also an awareness that holds us back. The country that we dream of demands gradualism, commitment, patience, and sacrifices. It can be built only day by day. It doesn't just come about by chance; the gods of the nations don't hold lotteries. They watch, they judge, and they reward. They also punish when they recognize defiance.

To arrive at our long-dreamed-of Italy, we've frequently taken dangerous shortcuts. Some people have suggested abandoning the euro, objecting to the interference of the European Union (only to turn around and complain that the European Union isn't doing enough for us). Others have justified the practice of systematic tax evasion while simultaneously complaining about the shortfalls in public services. Others still have stripped the school system of resources and then proceeded to bemoan that system's growing weaknesses. There are those who extend and slow down trials and then protest the law's delay. And then, of course, we've heard some people inciting public opinion against Covid vaccination, even though vaccination is what got us out of the mess in the first place.

The marks left by these excursions into recklessness remain visible, unfortunately. A survey carried out at the end of 2020 suggested that four out of ten Italians would be unwilling to receive a vaccination. That's hard to believe. And in fact, it wasn't true: there was a general rush for vaccines in 2021, also because of the Green Pass requirement to go to work, travel, or access most public places. We Italians are gifted with vivid imaginations, it's true. But we're not stupid.

10. Because in time we let our resentments go

Italy is a litigious machine with one distinctive characteristic: the engine of resentment, from time to time, sputters to a halt. Our ideological clashes are persistent and enduring, but our quibbles are frequently superficial and can be overcome with relative ease either by reconciliation or else by the outbreak of some new and different squabble. We suffer from therapeutic cases of amnesia. The tendency to forget in a hurry may complicate our relationship with history, but it also greases our social interactions. Quarreling is exhausting, basically. And after a while, we get tired of it.

In this aspect, we're different from other cultures. Especially American culture. Resentments last longer in the United States of America, rivalries are more deeply rooted, and divisions—political, cultural, and ethnic—appear to be deeper. Recent years have been marked by an unmistakable backsliding, especially for a nation built on the idea of cooperation among different peoples and traditions.

I read Malcolm Gladwell's *Talking to Strangers*. It starts out with the suicide of Sandra Bland, a bright and promising young African American woman from Chicago, in the aftermath of a Texas police stop gone wrong. "Prejudice and incompetence go a long way toward explaining social dysfunction in the United States. . . . There are bad cops. There are biased cops. Conservatives prefer the former interpretation, liberals the latter. In the end the two sides canceled each other out," wrote Gladwell.

At the root of the problem is an attitude: the attitude of the police toward citizens and the attitude of citizens toward the police. The situation in Italy is different and—may I say it?—better.

If we look to the past, there's no reason for it to be like that. Italian mistrust of authority—any and all authority—is deeprooted, systematic, and universal. Yet in our recent history, there's nothing comparable to the insurrection prompted by the murder of George Floyd or the revolts that ensued all across the United States, with concomitant deaths and injuries.

What are the explanations of this difference? Let me toss out a couple. The police and the carabinieri in Italy take a more conciliatory approach: to be pulled over by a squad car on an Italian street is a very different experience from being pulled over on an American one. In the Italian case, you talk (to excess at times); in the American case, it's best to keep quiet and obey instructions to the letter. Handcuffs, arrests, and body searches are not uncommon consequences of a traffic violation in the United States. In Italy, such outcomes are vanishingly rare.

The second explanation has to do with the enormous availability of weapons in the United States and the resulting consequences (in 2020, the number of murders in Chicago alone was three times that in all of Italy for the same year). This ensures that every encounter between police and civilians in the United States is unpredictable. The police are on edge and, not surprisingly, suspicious; in the face of the wrong sort of reaction, they can turn aggressive.

In Italy tensions aren't quite as high—not on the streets, not in the cities. Let's not minimize the abuses that occur here, though—beatings in police custody do happen, unfortunately, and often the victims are people of color. Let's not forget that the Mafia is Sicilian and various organized crime families threaten, maim, and kill fellow Italians—from Sicily to Campania, from Calabria to Puglia. We have plenty of criminals of our own, in other words. But everyday life in Italy is untouched by the tension and the resentments that are all too often hard to miss in the United States.

Italian politicians ought to take a lesson from this situation and do what they can to pour oil on troubled waters whenever they can. Constant bickering, in fact, is exhausting; endless controversy is unpleasant. Overdo it and you'll wear out your welcome. *Neque semper arcum tendit Apollo*—"Not even Apollo keeps his bow always bent"—wrote Horace (*Odes*, II, 10, 19). If Apollo can't do it, why should Matteo Salvini, Giorgia Meloni, and the array of other Italian populists who still mourn the defeat of Donald Trump? The decision to transform a stance of political opposition into a form of trench warfare may be a legitimate one, but it comes with consequences. No country can go on arguing incessantly.

11. Because we're self-critical, as long as we don't become self-defeating

Must we always and only say good things about Italy? Is verbal patriotism entirely compatible with good journalism? The answer is simple: no and again, no. If you love your country—even if you love someone else's country—that's understandable, but you're authorized to criticize it, constructively. If it's your job to report on a country, you should try to be objective in that reporting. "My country, right or wrong" may sound very fine, but it works less well in practice unless you're a diplomat, a soldier, or a member of the presidential cabinet.

I tried to remember these considerations after skimming through the readers' comments on an op-ed piece I published in the *New York Times*. The article was headlined "Why No One Goes to Naples," and it described—with a note of sadness—the missed opportunities of the tourist industry in southern Italy.

It started out like this: "Spring is here. In southern Italy, the sun is shining, the sky is blue and the weather is balmy. Orange blossom fragrances mingle with wafts of jasmine. The food is good, the wine is inexpensive, the locals are friendly and beauty is all around. But where are the tourists?" The tourists, I explained, do arrive; but in small numbers. Seven years ago, only 13 percent of foreign visitors ventured south of Rome. Has the percentage changed since then? Sadly, it has not: foreign visitors to Italy have increased in number (from forty-eight million to sixty-three million, a fifth of whom are Germans). But still, only a small percentage of them venture south of Rome. The long-term aftereffects of Covid are not likely to help matters.

In the past forty years we've dropped from first place to fifth in the ranking of world tourist destinations; we have only just restored our Ministry of Tourism, abolished years ago; the web portal italia.it was a costly, predictable disaster; the Italian Government Tourist Board spends a substantial chunk of its resources on salaries and administrative expenses; allowing individual regions of Italy to do their own promotions of tourism has only produced duplication of efforts and waste, such as the pharaonic headquarters of the Campania region in Manhattan (mercifully shut down in 2009).

Need I continue?

In a single week, just before I wrote that opinion piece, the airports of Germany saw 223 flights take off for the Balearic Islands (Mallorca, Menorca, Ibiza, and Formentera) and only seventeen flights take off for southern Italy. I know that some regions do better than others; Puglia, for instance. But numbers don't lie, and the facts are as I've outlined them. We don't talk much about it in Italy, because any serious discussion would force us to examine our consciences. What infrastructure and what services do we offer our guests? What medical assistance, what hospitals? What streets, what ports, how many airports, what railways? Taking a train from Puglia to Calabria is like traveling in the twentieth century: a sunkissed Italy, lacking transportation links, largely isolated, that seems straight out of a neorealist film.

I'd be sorry if any southern Italian readers drew the conclusion that I was in any way hostile to the South. Because I'm not. I love Italy, all of Italy, and I think I've made that clear in all my years of traveling and reporting.

So I'm not supposed to write or say certain things outside

Italy? Why on earth not? Out of love of my homeland? That's an ambiguous expression. What kind of love? If you love someone, you tell them straight, the way things actually are. You don't turn your back on them, pretending you can't see what's going on.

And what about people who warn not to wash your dirty laundry in public? How hypocritical. People who say this—everywhere—as often as not simply do not wash their dirty laundry at all and walk around emanating a distinct body odor. But dirty laundry needs washing, and then it needs to be hung out to dry in good, strong sunlight.

12. Because many speak, some listen, but everyone understands

I still remember the video. It depicted the French philosopher Alain Finkielkraut as he came dangerously close to being beaten up in a public street in Paris in February 2019. The mob—wearing yellow vests, helmets, face masks, and sunglasses—were following and berating him:

"France belongs to us!"

"Filthy Jew!"

"The people will punish you."

That was not merely a disgusting but isolated episode; it was an alarm that should sound painfully loud in our ears. Anyone who fails to hear has chosen to ignore it. Any open display of anti-Semitism that takes place without consequences is shocking and deplorable. And that statement, echoed repeatedly, should leave us breathless. "We are the people." Says who? Since when can an aggressive minority claim for itself the right to pass itself off as "the people"? If we let them, sooner or later, they will become a majority. And at that point, anything can happen. In any country in Europe.

In fact, it has happened in the past.

I happened to be talking to a Frenchman who runs a major Italian corporation with headquarters in Rome. He, like me, was astonished by the broadside of gratuitous attacks that the Italian government—at that time a coalition between the League and the Five Star Movement—was unleashing against France. But he was expounding a theory that I found unconvincing: "The violent protests of the Yellow Vests are a sign of the French personality, while the absence of such clashes in Italy only points to your resignation." Not so, I told him. The nonviolent aren't resigned; they're farsighted. Italy possesses a strange wisdom. Imitate us, rather than pretending to be proud of your mistakes.

But we Italians should also be careful. The opposition between "the elites" and "the people" is not a uniquely French one. It's not a harmless parlor game. It's not an outdated parody of "the class struggle." It's not just another desperate attempt to feel as if one is "on the side of the masses" (certain rusty old hulks on the historic left never give up, and they look for homes in the most improbable locations). It can't even become a clever electoral simplification. Let's leave certain experiments to the British and the Americans, keeping in mind what they produced: Brexit and Trump. Let's just hope that they turn out to be bumps on a road to elsewhere.

The idea of exploiting the force, the rage, and often the naiveté of the masses goes back to ancient times. From Tiberius Gracchus to Nicolás Maduro, with stops along the way for some of the most tragic experiences of all mankind: Nazism, communism, fascism. The process is invariably the same: stir up discontent and fear among the populace; inflame the ordinary people against the governing class (politicians, businessmen, cultural leaders); replace that governing class, becoming the new elite yourself; make yourself irreplaceable, at least until the next traumatic upheaval. Just think of what the Soviet Union became after its bloody birth as a revolt of the people against the czars. Just think of what became of Boris Yeltsin's Russia after it emerged as a reaction to the Soviet Union. And just think of what Vladimir Putin's Russia has become, long after its birth as a reaction to Boris Yeltsin's Russia.

Certainly, the new European populists can hardly be

compared to Vladimir Lenin or Benito Mussolini (though I wouldn't trust some of them as far as I could throw them). But the mechanisms that they use, the emotions they play upon, and the slogans they adopt, unfortunately, are reminiscent. The dichotomy "people versus elites"—we can't say it too often—is a fraud. We're all people—we all vote, we all experience the consequences of our actions—and we all ought to be able to become elites. In other words, to become successful: a farsighted businessman is a member of the elite, a brilliant engineer is a member of the elite, a competent mayor is a member of the elite, a sharp-eyed publisher is a member of the elite, a talented craftsman is a member of the elite, and an academic who knows how to study deeply and teach capably is a member of the elite.

When a democracy is healthy, it becomes a form of osmosis: it allows mobility through the ranks of society. The dichotomy of people versus elites, in contrast, is unhealthy. It engenders frustration, it glorifies sacrifice, it justifies aggression, and it humiliates the capable and competent. Is this what we want in Italy? I don't think so. Certainly, there are experts and professionals who are arrogant and off-putting, and they become the targets of eminently justified critiques; we'll talk about them later. But to transform this resentment into a large political project is deplorable and shameful.

In Italy, many speak, some listen, but everyone—deep down—understands. Maybe I'm laboring under an illusion, but I have the feeling that the great majority is well aware of the great risk we're running. And that they'll know how to avoid it.

13. Because every so often, we do embarrassing things, and we know it

The uses and abuses of chat rooms and WhatsApp groups during a pandemic would be a fantastic subject for a film. We could borrow the title, with apologies, from the director Paolo Genovese, but with a twist: instead of *Perfect Strangers*, we could call it *Imperfect Familiars*. Many of our friends and relatives have confirmed everything we already knew about them. For starters, they doused us with questionable wisecracks, cartoons, and memes; then they started spreading anxieties and fears (that too is a form of pandemic infection). Or else showing off excesses of chauvinism: their own city or region as a paragon for the world to admire, the cities or regions of others as a target of derision, or worse.

Some people are still doing it.

Their conversations and social media profiles seemed to have assigned themselves a mission: to frighten others and to frighten themselves. Their emotions bubbled over, their omens proliferated, their obsessions sprouted as fast as the weeds in neglected flowerbeds. The fault is not with the medium, the fault is with the message. Facebook and WhatsApp helped doctors and nurses stay afloat in a sea of uncertainty; they helped families and couples ripped apart by the lockdown to maintain ties and organize their lives; they helped corporations to recalibrate and deploy their workforce; they helped people living alone to feel a little less lonely.

For other Italians, social media has been, and remains, a playground; the various communities in the chat rooms are a sort of open city where all is fair and anything is permitted. In the specific case of the pandemic, they facilitated the spread of any and all sorts of news, indifferent to the panic and alarm it might instill. But there are communities and groups of all sorts, as we know: classrooms, offices, newsrooms, associations; cycling hobbyists, five-a-side soccer players, professional soccer fans. Often they overdo things: snark, stupid pranks, wisecracks worthy of pimply teenagers, or even worse: obscenities, racist and misogynistic memes (with pictures attached). In the old days, we talked about locker room humor. Nowadays, in the locker rooms, people refer to chat room humor.

Some of you may be thinking, the real crimes that occur online are far more serious: child pornography, narcotics and weapons trafficking, sexual harassment, fraud, and systematic slander and defamation. True enough. But those are acts that can be punished with legal sanctions, not statements that are socially awkward and deplorable. Condemning the former doesn't mean giving a free pass to the latter.

No one is calling for a nation embalmed in propriety. But there are certain collective habits that denote a careless, superficial approach. And we're not a superficial people. We are a nation, however, that has an unfortunate tendency to absolve itself of blame. That absolution comes after a hasty examination of our conscience, in a process that sees us simultaneously playing the roles of defendant, witness, prosecutor, attorney for the defense, and judge.

You can just guess how *that* will turn out.

14. Because when we speak a lot, we say very little— and the other way around

I went to China at the end of 2019, before anyone was talking about Covid. Beijing, Guangzhou (Canton), Shenzhen, and Hong Kong. I had been invited as part of the XIX Week of the Italian Language in the World. In the universities that I visited, I tried to explain Italy through the following key words: *Ah!*—*Bah!*—*Be'?*—*Boh!*—*Eh!*—*Eh . . . ?*—*Mah!*—*Oh!* All told, nineteen letters.

1. *Ah!* indicates the joy of understanding, the satisfaction of seeing one's hunch confirmed. We Italians are notoriously fond of hunches, perhaps a little too fond—so much so that we frequently forget to delve deeper. Really, we ought to. That, too, can be a pleasure.

2. *Bah!* indicates distaste, irritation, and even disgust. Any political argument in Italy is bound to feature at least two *Bah!*s, complete with exclamation marks. In fact, Italian voters expect very little from their candidates, so they try to limit their feelings of disappointment. The British, in contrast, expect a great deal from their politicians; that's why the poor management of Brexit traumatized them so deeply.

3. *Be'?* Translation: "So now what?" It's an annoyed demand for information, and it highlights two na-

tional traits: curiosity and impatience. Our national impatience is a foundation upon which the various parties build their election strategies: Promise something right away. What about the future? Well, that's posterity's problem.

4. *Boh!* is a very brisk way of saying "I couldn't say." Perhaps the most concise philosophical treatise currently in circulation.

5. *Eh!* Translation: "There, I told you so." It's not great form to be openly dismissive of other people's disappointments. But doing so can be so strangely satisfying at times.

6. *Eh . . . ?* indicates astonishment, disbelief. Matteo: "I heard Donald Trump has become humble!" Enrico: "Eh . . . ?"

7. *Mah!* is a sigh, an exhalation dense with concern. There's a proverb, *"Chi dice 'mah!,' cuor contento non ha."* (Anyone who says *Mah!* is probably downhearted.) These three letters should be incorporated into the Italian Constitution. Article 140: *Mah!*

8. *Oh!* "Depending on how it is uttered, *Oh!* can express various emotions: sorrow, pain, indignation, boredom, astonishment, pleasure, and desire." Thus speaks the Treccani dictionary. It's a matter of tonality, then. In that field, of course, the Chinese have no need to take lessons from us. Mandarin has four or five tones, Cantonese between six and ten.

It's harder to learn the array of gestures that accompany these Italian expressions. Certain movements of the head, certain contortions of the fingers, certain jerks of the forearm are the products of history, wits, and exercises of concision. Still, in the Italian Studies Departments of Beijing, Guangzhou, and Hong Kong, we certainly worked on it. Just ask the people there what the post-Covid world will look like. They will reply "Boh!" while throwing both arms wide, just like real Italians.

15. Because we may not all be poets, but we recognize poetry

I adore prejudices, commonplace cliches
I like to think that in Holland
there are still children wearing wooden shoes
that in Naples they play the mandolin
that you're waiting for me with an undertone of anxiety
as I change trains between Lambrate and Garibaldi.

The author of these lines is Luciano Erba, a Milanese poet who lived from 1922 to 2010. The title of the poem is "Linea lombarda" ("Lombard Line"), and it comes from the collection *Nella terra di mezzo* (*In the Middle Ground*, 2000). Once you know that Lambrate and Garibaldi are two subway stations in Milan, no further explanation is required.

Poetry picks a corner of reality shrouded in penumbra and illuminates it. We focus our eyes, and we understand. It takes very little. Even the experience of changing Metro trains in Milan summons up memories and emotions.

Poetry belongs not only to those who write it but also to those who read it and listen to it. It proceeds through subterranean channels; it surfaces in society and then dives away out of sight, and never randomly. My feeling is that poetry emerges in moments of crisis and transition—look at Amanda Gorman's impact on Americans. It's as if that's when people feel the need to understand more deeply and clearly, to find a shaft of sunlight in the dark forest of current events. Poetry has this ability. It offers a lightning synthesis that reaches the brain by way of the heart.

The turn of the 2020s, the third decade of the twenty-first

century, is reminiscent of the beginning of the 1970s, the eighth decade of the twentieth century and a time of great political, economic, and social uncertainty. Then and now, the Italians wanted change, their impatience generated confusion, that confusion produced uncertainty, and that uncertainty demanded consolation. Poetry provided it. We must turn once again to poetry for the help it can provide in the aftermath of a pandemic.

Fifty years ago, the need for poetry was assuaged, in part, with songs by, among others, Lucio Battisti, Fabrizio De André, and Francesco Guccini (listen to them, they'll help you understand us). But there also existed a thriving poetry scene, and I have proof of that fact in my home. Aldo Borlenghi—a poet, critic, and philologist, a personal friend of the poets Giuseppe Ungaretti and Vittorio Sereni—married an aunt of mine, Franca Severgnini, who worked as a pharmacist. My apartment in Milan was their home before it became mine, and a virtual library of the Italian Novecento was handed down to me. All sorts of things pop out of it; it's a veritable gold mine of serendipity, where I continually find things I never thought to look for.

A few years ago, while making a public appearance, I made the acquaintance of a man in his midseventies, Brianza born and raised. He'd come to the event specifically to talk to me. As a young man, he had studied at the Istituto Tecnico Carlo Cattaneo, where my Tuscan-born uncle, Borlenghi, who'd come to Milan from Switzerland (to which he'd been exiled by the Fascists), had been given a teaching position. The old man told me, "Your uncle had us read poetry in class. At first we made fun of him. Today I say: for many of us, it changed our lives."

It's not only a lovely way to commemorate a teacher as well as a delicate tribute to poetry; it's also a useful reminder: even

now, we all need evocative food for thought. Poetry is almost
never a bestseller, and it's rarely heard on the radio or seen
on television; only social media has offered it a scrap of the
space it deserves. But when poetry does appear—pulled out of
a bookshelf, declaimed on a piazza, tucked into a dedication or
a text message—the Italians recognize it instantly. It's as if our
long years of familiarity with it—twenty-three centuries, if
we count the language we spoke before Italian—have created
an unconscious sensibility. We're a nation of poetic apathists,
and we continue to surprise: the world, but first and foremost
ourselves.

⸙

I've never been able to pin down the source of my passion
for Trieste. I wasn't born there, I didn't study there, I haven't
worked there, I never fell in love while strolling along Via XX
Settembre or lying in the sun at Barcola. But when I hear
"Triéste"—with the first *e* uttered elongated and narrow, like
the eyes of the city's young women—I freeze. I listen, l look, I
read, and I want to understand.

   Why does Trieste attract me so powerfully? Is it because it's
so very Italian, so decidedly Austrian, and so notably Slavic?
Because it's Jewish, Roman Catholic, and Eastern Orthodox?
Because it's the North of the South, the South of the North,
the East of the West, and the West of the East? No, or not only.
Trieste attracts me because it's a poetic city. Rome, Naples,
Venice, and Florence are theatrical cities; well aware of their
beauty, they show themselves off. Milan, Turin, Bari, and Palermo are narrative cities: machines made to build plotlines.
Trieste, like Genoa and Cagliari, is poetic. And poetry pops
up everywhere: from a nook or a corner, from a steep uphill

street, from a boulevard, from the many sails of the Barcolana regatta that light up in unison in the bright sunlight.

At home, my books of Italian fiction and poetry are arranged alphabetically by author. With one exception: writers and poets from Trieste. Italo Svevo, Umberto Saba, Giani Stuparich, Scipio Slataper, Pier Antonio Quarantotti Gambini, Fulvio Tomizza, Claudio Magris, and all the others are slapped chaotically together. Every so often I challenge them: come on, reveal to me the secret of your incredible city. Why does Trieste hypnotize outsiders, who forgive it everything, and impassion the Triestines, who forgive it nothing?

And so when I saw the title, *La città celeste*, and the painting on the cover, I recognized it immediately, my geographic obsession. The book was published in 2021. The author is Diego Marani, a translator and linguist. Born in Ferrara, he studied in Trieste and spent many years in Brussels. In my mind, I called him out, as if challenging him to a duel. *Go ahead*, I thought, *try to explain to me the inexplicable.*

Reader, he did it. *La città celeste* is a coming-of-age story. But the experiences of the main character—his father, anguished and anguishing, an apartment on Via San Nicolò, the study of languages, love stories with two Slovenian women in succession (the blonde Vesna and the brunette Jasna, sisters)— are merely garnishes, side dishes. The main course is Trieste herself, a mixture of peoples, seafront and highland, port and railroad: a mental terminus. Repeatedly, with a sniper's precision, Marani hits a definition dead center, making me feel just like him: "A test-tube Triestine, the only one in the whole city not waging some lawsuit against Trieste, not harboring a grudge, without a score to settle."

"[Trieste] always seems to be on a fold in the map," wrote Jan Morris, one of the authors who knew the city best and understood it most thoroughly. In *Trieste and the Meaning of Nowhere* (2001)—her last book, after which she never wrote another—ends with these words: "Here more than anywhere I remember lost times, lost chances, lost friends, with the sweet tristesse that is onomatopoeic to the place." She's right. Trieste has a scent of lost possibilities and opportunities. It's a place where angels brush past you.

"Cities are women, and it's possible to fall in love with them, too, and never forget them," Diego Marani concluded. That's true, and every Italian knows it without anyone ever having to teach us.

16. Because many of us have been fortunate in life, and we know it

The photograph emerged from the forest of Facebook. Spring 1982. There I am in my uniform, my arms clasping the shoulders of two fellow draftees from the military motor pool. I'm pretending to collapse to the ground while they hold me upright. There was just one month left till the end of our mandatory military service. My hair was dark, and that's predictable. But my trousers were black, too, and in the Italian Air Force you'd expect them to be sky blue. It was an indication that, with just one month left till we became free men, we were doing more or less as we pleased: mop of hair, uniform jacket, and jeans. We looked like a Po Valley version of Duran Duran, not three draftees in the barracks. Even military conscription was a movable feast for many of us; an extended chapter of our adolescence, kindly imposed upon us by the Italian government.

I came into this world on December 26, 1956. My birth year places me squarely at the center of the generation of what came to be known as baby boomers, conventionally bookended by the years 1946 and 1966. The term originated in the United States, but it's familiar everywhere around the world. We boomers are the children of the postwar economic boom. The Americans likewise dubbed our parents' generation, born in the first third of the twentieth century, the generation that lived through fascism, Nazism, and communism, a long war and a challenging postwar: the Greatest Generation. A superlative they deserved, I'd say.

Well, then, if our fathers and mothers were born into the greatest generation, we were the luckiest generation. Those of us born in the West experienced no wars. Just think: no one, in the history of mankind, had ever enjoyed such immense privilege.

We grew up in a society that was virtually bathed in optimism. The recovery was driven by technology and advertising (I'd suggest the television series *Mad Men* if you want to study the period in the United States); our recovery coincided with the development of the European Economic Community (the Treaty of Rome was signed in 1957). The postwar recovery created a psychological, social, and economic springboard. In Italy, there was suddenly plenty of work available, electric appliances, paid vacations and vaccinations, opportunities and new outlooks. If a father and a mother know that they are doing better today than they were yesterday, and if they can assume that things will be even better for their children tomorrow, they are going to be happy, and that will be felt by everyone in their home. That was the atmosphere in the families of the 1950s and the early '60s. They brushed our hair into embarrassing styles and dressed us like oversized dolls. But it isn't a quiff, a ribbon, nor a school smock that marks your personality.

Our personalities were shaped by the idea that almost everything was possible; a naive idea, I'll give you that. But optimistic naiveté is better than precocious skepticism. Some generations came up against precisely that early embitterment. Think of our children, the millennials, born at the end of the twentieth century. They weren't at fault, any more than we deserve any kind of credit. The history of humanity is a journey, but we don't get to choose which stage of that long voyage we'll be traveling.

Fortune smiled on the luckiest generation even during our youth. It's true that in Italy and other European countries, we encountered homegrown terrorism: an outburst of criminal idiocy, a deplorable mess. But it was possible to sidestep it. We had love, friends, travel, and sports. And politics in those years didn't necessarily have to be violent. For many of us, it was even an exercise in patience, a playing field of tolerance, a test of method and character. Student political assemblies were rites of passage. Have you ever wondered why so many boomers are comfortable speaking into a microphone? Because we learned to do it in a madhouse, while that one special person was watching us from the fifth row with a smile on their face. Anyone who can make it through an ordeal of that kind can face anything life throws at them: a conference, a business meeting, a news conference. Even a condo board meeting.

Our good fortune also extended to other sectors, no less important. Our older brothers and sisters—the senior boomers, now in their seventies—had the Beatles, the Rolling Stones, and Bob Dylan. We, their younger brothers and sisters, grew up with "Let It Be" (1970)—perfect for slow dancing, which wasn't actually dancing at all but a chaste form of sexual foreplay—Pink Floyd, Genesis, and King Crimson. And, of course, Neil Young. Play "Out on the Weekend" or "Harvest" to people age sixty-five and they'll melt like butter on popcorn. What about in Italy? The names mentioned previously: Lucio Battisti, Fabrizio De André, Francesco Guccini.

And then there was sex: a delightful obsession, and it wasn't limited to the mental sphere. What distinguished us from the generations that preceded us? The opportunity to experiment, which, as any scientist can tell you, means the following: try and try again, without disastrous consequences. We were the world champions of sexual sophistry and self-indulgence. The oldest among us shattered familial, social, and religious barricades, whereas we, born in the late 1950s and the early '60s, found the road ahead perfectly clear. For any gender, it wasn't an abrupt transgression; instead, it was the beginning of a series of loving explorations. We excelled in erotic relativism, which no other generation has experienced, neither before nor after. Our parents were restricted by guilty feelings and social disapproval; those who came after us had to deal with AIDS, which changed the way everyone behaved.

Our good luck didn't end there. The luckiest generation entered the working world between the late 1960s and the late 1980s, when employers offered cast-iron contracts, not will-o'-the-wisp compliments. Not everyone, I should point out, found happiness, either professional or economic. Many, I have the impression, were led astray by the intoxicating sensation of being able to do anything we pleased. We mistook recklessness for courage, overweening ambition for plans, presumption for passion. I feel safe stating, though, that every one of us absorbed certain mental attitudes that might not have led to great careers and impressive results but still marked our personalities: antiauthoritarianism, for instance, the idea that an order must be reasonable and the expectation—forgive me, the *illusion*—that those in charge must earn that position.

Our generational streak of good luck continued on through the '90s, which for many of us was a time of new families and demographic maturity. That period was marked, in nearly all Western countries, by a sort of truce: geopolitical, economic, and psychological. In the middle of that decade the internet entered our lives, but most people failed even to notice it at first and grasped its impact only in the new century. At that point many of us—though not all—were able to make the best of it, rediscovering in the aughts a mental, professional, and personal vitality that they were afraid we'd lost. Various disasters ensued, especially in the realm of personal relations, but nothing that previous generations hadn't gotten up to in the past, even though they had lacked Facebook and WhatsApp to help them on their way.

The 2010s are still too close behind us, and the 2020s still too new, to be able to measure their impact on one's own generation. It hasn't been an easy period, that much we know: the economy never fully recovered from the beating it took in 2008 and 2009. Terrorism, various forms of excess, and fanaticism have marked our politics and our news. Here, too, however, if you stop to think about it, the luckiest generation has shown that it deserves its name. Those upheavals came along when the boomers were in their fifties and sixties, after their lives, families, and livelihoods were already well established; after their failures and disappointments—who hasn't had those?— had been fully digested; at a time when age helps—or ought to help—to put things into proper perspective. The time has come to help those who come after us: children, grandchildren, students, colleagues, and younger friends. At the risk of seeming paternalistic, it's true. But warding off that sense of futility that marks the third chapter of so many lives.

And that, of course, is the luckiest thing about being lucky: being able to give back during a transition like this one, a period that is anything but easy and is not, sadly, over. The ultimate consequences of Covid are impossible to estimate at present. But these are the times when the calm derived from experience is especially pertinent and we Italian boomers can make ourselves useful. There's no need to be heroes. It's enough just to take a look around. It's enough to realize that we came after someone else and that someone else will come after us.

Serving a purpose: what a wonderful thing. Generosity is a form of power, people say. But a lack of generosity is a form of stupidity. And that's far worse.

17. Because our children see the future, and now and then they explain it to us

The term *innovation* tends to stir up justifiable mistrust. We Italians have abused it in recent years. There hasn't been a single organization, association, corporation, university, cultural circle, spiritual group, or political movement that hasn't flaunted it. Innovation! Transformation! Renewal! Rebirth! Refoundation! Everyone wants to innovate, and that's fitting and proper, at least in theory. Change is a healthy reaction to the aging of individuals and institutions. So what's the problem? Often, innovation is nothing more than a proclamation followed by little or no action.

Things haven't changed even now that change has imposed itself forcibly: the economic recession that's come on the heels of the pandemic leaves us no alternative. *Innovation* is by now a term of fashion, repeated obsessively—like *protest* in the 1960s, *movement* in the 1970s, *development* in the 1980s, *ethics* in the 1990s, *governance* in the aughts, and *sustainability* in the 2010s. It's something that happens with words: they become so common that their meaning fades into the background. What matters is the light they cast.

The only people who show any real respect for the concept of innovation are those who fear it. And in Italy, that's quite a lot of people. You can call them conservatives, traditionalists, resisters, or even reactionaries; they hunker down in the world of politics and in corporations, in government offices and in schools, in the media and in society. Perhaps they don't understand that *innovation* is a learned term, derived from late Latin and first used in the fourteenth century, but they fear its consequences, and they know what it means:

(a)   a modification that entails elements of the new ("making innovations in a system")
(b)   a new element ("there are several innovations in the system")

A frequent impediment to innovation is age. My mother, Mamma Carla, fought epic battles with every new gadget, especially tape recorders, which she used in the 1970s and '80s to learn English. My father, Papà Angelo, at age ninety-five, scrolled through his iPad with an easy, intuitive movement, but he loathed and detested the new remote control of his satellite television and insisted on writing the instructions on a sheet of paper, a process that soon became even more challenging than working the remote. I detest our new thermostats; I don't understand them. (Does the snowflake mean heating or cooling?) Most of us, having reached a certain age—two-thirds of the average life span?—start to become annoyed with the continual demands to change, update, and renew.

Conservatives are almost invariably frightened human beings. It is impossible to accept a lifetime of innovation. But it's irresponsible to reject it too soon or just out of some preconceived position. Let's stay with technology. The demise of the instruction manual was a traumatic transition for many (even though the onscreen commands and online information are clearer and more convenient). The disappearance of jacks and cables, replaced by Wi-Fi, has been a surprise. I remember that the absence of USB ports on the new MacBook Air struck me as an act of insolence, or perhaps a cunning piece of marketing. Let's face it: Apple knows a thing or two about cunning pieces of marketing (shall we talk about the price of a charger these days?). But the MacBook update doesn't fall into this category. It was time for that update, and soon we all realized it.

Why did I accept that new development, along with a great many others? Why does the technology of the present day not frighten me? Why does the race toward artificial intelligence make me stop to think but doesn't terrify me? First of all, because I understand that nearly all generations have faced demanding challenges: steam power, electric energy, the telephone, television. My grandfather Giuseppe (1881–1954) was a farmer, and when he needed to come into the town of Crema, he hitched up the horses to his gig. Later he learned to drive a car. Now, that was a heroic transformation. Figuring out how to use Google Maps? Not so much.

Some of you may wonder: Is there a way to buffer the trauma of technological innovation? Or perhaps of innovation in general? Maybe there is: stay close to people who are unafraid of change, and experience it with comfort and ease. Those are almost always people younger than we are.

If I am writing this, if I'm able to use my iPhone with a certain dignity, if Ortensia and I live in a comfortable and reasonably technologically advanced house, the credit goes entirely to our son, Antonio, who was born in 1992. Ever since he became a teenager, our dinners—at first every evening and now whenever he drops by to see us, criticizing the choice of menu—have been refresher courses of all sorts. For our part, we tried to explain the complexities of grown-up life to him; he managed to clear up some of the mysteries of digital life for us. During the first lockdown, which we spent together, I offered breaking political and health news; he downloaded new apps and provided commentary.

It was a mutually beneficial arrangement.

Antonio explains (when he feels like it), exhibits and shows (gladly), and solves problems (almost always): how to hook up the TV soundbar, how to manage pictures on Apple Photos, how to use the Volvo's instrument panel, how to watch TV shows on Sky Go, everything from Amazon to the electric scooter and from Netflix to Apple TV; he does his best to be helpful and clear, and he never loses his temper with us. Since he runs a restaurant, he even has useful tips and explanations about our household appliances: when our refrigerator stopped maintaining a reliable temperature, he issued an expert opinion (replace it). For the sake of our image and parental dignity, my wife and I do our best to keep up with him. We watch, we ask, we try to understand. Our son distributes information, praise, and critiques with great equanimity. Here's the outcome: I now do better with my smartphone than Ortensia does with hers. As for everything else—television set, electric kettle, Wi-Fi, home banking—she's much more capable than I am. Oh, I was forgetting one thing: ten years ago, my wife was so fond of her little brick of a Nokia cell phone that she refused to switch to an iPhone. If I tried to hide her iPhone from her now, she'd divorce me.

I've found other sources of advice and expertise in my nieces, younger friends and colleagues, and my students. Turning to people of another generation is not just a way of giving back and a genuine pleasure; it's also an investment. Innovation for people in their twenties or thirties requires no effort; it's just part of life. When you're young, change comes naturally.

That became clear during the pandemic, which forced families to adopt new modes of communication in order to keep up with the news, learn and study, go shopping, talk to and see each other, work out, and take yoga or exercise lessons. "Digital transition" is suddenly no longer the title of a conference or a government commission. And who deserves the credit for that? A new generation of Italians, who scoffed at the challenges and made life easier for everybody.

It's a normal, healthy form of cooperation, yet many seem not to understand it. The various generations are complementary; each group can provide something that the other lacks: energy, imagination, and flexibility on the one hand; experience and the ability to sum up matters on the other. I see evidence of this win-win situation all the time: working with people half one's age is a blessing.

Teachers do learn at a certain age.

18. Because we can have fun without getting filthy drunk

My youth was unfettered by aperitifs. In the '70s, we focused on discotheques, warm beer on the beach, pizza, sleepless nights with our friends, and cheap wine; we didn't expect much. Aperitifs were for older people: our parents, our parents' friends, our aunts, and our uncles. Especially when they were on vacation. But when we had guests over, our dining room suddenly dotted with bottles filled with brightly colored liquids with funny names: Aperol, Campari, Carpano, Fernet-Branca. In the TV commercial for Cynar, an actor sipped the artichoke-flavored aperitif while stuck in traffic: "Against the wear and tear of modern life!" A popular brand of vermouth was Punt e Mes, which means "a point and a half" (a point of sweetness, half a point of bitterness). At age twenty I'd have gladly died rather than order a Punt e Mes. No girl I knew would have been seen with me if I had.

The national habit of the aperitif—in Italian, *aperitivo*, a drink enjoyed in the company of others at the beginning of an evening—was imported from the United States and the United Kingdom, places that dictated fashions and social trends in Italy during the first half of the twentieth century. Paolo Monelli, in his book *Optimus Potor ossia il vero bevitore* (1935), wrote, "The custom has spread rapidly throughout Italy, especially since the Great War, of serving alcoholic beverages made up of varied ingredients, generally known as 'cocktails.'" The Fascist regime, which held power in Italy from 1922 until 1943, detested the bourgeois Anglo-Saxon drink and dubbed it "Harlequin beverage" (as in "particolored beverage" or "tutti-frutti beverage") or "polybeverage" or "multidrink." Obviously, the Fascist Party's attempt to rename the cocktail failed miserably. No one was interested in drinking polybeverages. As soon as Mussolini was overthrown, cocktails came back—with their proper name.

The 1950s and '60s were awash in *aperitivi*, especially among those who could afford them. After a pause between the 1970s and the '90s—our generation, as I was saying, preferred travel, music, and sex—the custom gained renewed vigor in the twenty-first century. The rule governing the *aperitivo* nowadays is a simple one: anyhow, anywhere, with anyone. North and South, big cities and small towns, the prosperous and the penniless, young people and parents, all of them have wholeheartedly converted to this new social practice (our grandparents, of course, never gave it up). When evening falls, the country of Italy, in every season of the year, turns into one single immensely long bar.

And the upshot? A new generation discusses alcoholic beverages with a passion that was once reserved for politics. Let's add this: the new Italian adults also drink wine at dinner, love restaurants, and shun discotheques, which have consequently slid into a state of crisis. Among the other outcomes is a drop in car crashes involving very young people. Italian millennials drink more, it's true, but compared with their counterparts at the end of the twentieth century, they drive far less.

The *aperitivo* has become the new pillar of Italian social life. And we have to admit that it offers a number of advantages. It's tactically intelligent, because it doesn't require people to spend the whole evening together. It's quite reasonably priced (from five to ten euros). And it comes in different formats. There's the basic *aperitivo*. There's the double-strength *aperitivo*, where the drinks come with some side dishes; and then there's the *apericena* (*aperitivo con cena*, drinks with dinner), which obviates the evening meal. None of this will come as news to any Italian who's socially active these days, but it may seem more arcane and obtuse to those who only occasionally practice this social rite. I know people in their sixties who spend the evening wondering *Should I eat everything (cold cuts, focaccia, minipizzas, cheeses, olives, pickled cucumbers, celery)? But then what if we go out to dinner? Or I could eat nothing. But then what if we* don't *go out to dinner?*

The spread of the *aperitivo* throughout Italian society has engendered curiosity and expertise. Young Italians frequently talk about flavors and combinations, for instance (apparently a gin and tonic goes nicely with a tuna carpaccio). British and American visitors to Italy take umbrage at this approach. They insist that aperitifs must be drunk without eating, to maximize their alcoholic impact. They forget one important detail: We Italians, as a rule, aren't out to get drunk. We just want to have fun together.

Some drinks are more popular than others. Prosecco has become a distinctive marker of the late afternoon, just as the cappuccino is emblematic of the Italian morning (after eleven o'clock, we consider a cappuccino to be immoral; after a meal, illegal). Prosecco is ubiquitous, a form of liquid democracy that unites different generations. It's also the base ingredient of the Spritz, a very popular *aperitivo* that originated in the Veneto region. It consists of prosecco, Aperol or Campari, and a shot of seltzer water (the name of the drink comes from the German verb *spritzen*, "to spray"). Trentino and Franciacorta (between Brescia and Lake Iseo) produce better bubblies, but the main brands—Ferrari, Bellavista, Ca' del Bosco, Berlucchi—have never been able to find a shared name for their excellent wines. In Italy, they're considered quite highly, but they've never managed to attain the kind of global dominion that prosecco enjoys. Say "Bellavista" to an American friend, and he'll think you're saying there's a lovely view. Offer a "Ferrari" to a Chinese friend, and he'll ask if he can drive it.

So is Italy a victim of prosecco populism? Let's not overstate. We are, however, an enological and gastronomical superpower, and when it comes to certain matters, we should consider carefully before discussing with outsiders. What drives politicians to appear on social media with a glass in their hand? Why, in the summer of 2019, did Matteo Salvini—at the time deputy prime minister and minister of the interior—perform a DJ set in Milano Marittima, with girls in bikinis shaking their hips to the tune of Italy's national anthem? It's not easy to answer that question (and not only because it's practically impossible to dance to the "Inno di Mameli" on the beach).

Perhaps it's best to advise our non-Italian friends to keep a safe distance from these locations. If you wish to study the universe of the *aperitivo*, the best you can do is just to spend time in any of the excellent bars in our cities or in the mountains, in the hills, at the seaside, along the rivers, or on the lakes. There are options of all kinds, for all ages and every pocketbook. Giving a visitor to Italy too much advice seems pushy.

In one of his short stories, titled "Il vino di Carema" ("The Wine of Carema"), Mario Soldati wrote, "If you want to enjoy yourself in Italy—I explain to my foreign friends—you need to discover it for yourself, trusting in your own good luck and your instincts, because a great and important law in Italy dictates this exact subject: here, in Italy, everything that has a title, a name, an advertisement, is inevitably much less valuable than everything that is unknown, hidden, individual."

Is it still that way? Think it over, without haste. Ideally over an *aperitivo*.

19. Because we care about *la bella figura,* but we also love *una bella risata* (a good laugh)

Lipstick index is a term coined by Leonard Lauder, the chairman emeritus of Estée Lauder. It was a way of explaining the sudden rise in sales during the recession of 2001. He thought cosmetics sales—especially of lipstick—were countercyclical. Thus, many women, in the challenging economic situation, consoled themselves by buying lipstick and putting off larger purchases.

During 2020 and 2021, things went differently. Sales of lipstick in Italy dropped by 70 percent, whereas mascara sales held up well. The explanation? A mask covers your mouth, not your eyes. And people who are stuck indoors use less lipstick. My hometown, Crema, is Italy's proud cosmetics capital; it produces a quarter of the world's mascara.

As long as we're on the subject of appearance: Why does a nation as esthetically obsessed as Italy treat its onscreen image with such indifference? Video calls, webinars, online birthday parties, distance teaching, television appearances: slovenliness is everywhere, and it's surprising. You don't have to be beautiful to appear on TV (otherwise, yours truly would stick to writing). But a modicum of attention to your onscreen image is a sign of respect for your audience, whatever your gender, whatever your age.

The things we're seeing! Television appearances in which the person being interviewed speaks in the dark, like the Grinch, or government undersecretaries turn a table lamp into their face, as if being grilled by the police. Talks to school groups where the students look like fashion models and the teachers look as if they just ran away from home. Journalists who speak with their nose pressed up against the lens, economists as out of focus as if they were ectoplasmic, epidemiologists who fill the screen with their epidermis. And how about the backgrounds of Skype conversations? Even though they know they're entering other people's homes, many speakers station themselves in apartment hallways or in corners between two armoires, or else the backgrounds feature unidentified household objects. (What are they? Statuettes from manger scenes, fitness equipment, instruments of torture?)

The spectacle is so stunning that a suspicion formed in my mind: Certain people who choose certain framings or backgrounds are neither careless nor preoccupied. They know exactly what they're doing. They're trying to increase the nation's good humor.

20. Because Milan is political and sensual

When I was a young man, Milan seemed as mysterious to me as Amazonia. I'd grown up in Crema, just thirty miles to the southeast; I'd studied at the University of Pavia and prepared my diploma thesis in Brussels. That vast, neighboring, concentric city—Milan had no large river, lots of traffic, just one skyscraper with an awkward nickname, "Pirellone"—instilled anxiety in me, a sensation shared by many of my fellow Cremaschi for generations. To natives of Crema eager to find their way out of the tentacular metropolis, the following advice was offered, in dialect: *"Vaga à dré a l'uselù"*—"Follow the big bird"—where the winged creature in question was the silhouette of an airplane on road signs pointing the way to Linate Airport. Once we reached Linate, we were out of danger. State Road 415 "Paullese," the Adda River, the countryside, the welcoming gates of Crema, back home safe and sound.

When the great journalist Indro Montanelli sent for me in 1980 after reading a few of my articles for the Cremona paper *La Provincia*, I had no alternative: I had to come back to Milan, a city that Signor Montanelli, born near Florence, loved deeply ("Italy will be a serious country only when it becomes Milanese," he used to say). I showed up late for my appointment in his office at 4 Via Gaetano Negri in the Cordusio neighborhood, on Friday, December 19, drenched to the bone (it was raining, it was cold out, I didn't know the city, I didn't have an umbrella, and I'd wandered around and around, searching for the address). I stood there, in front of the desk of the founder and editor in chief of *Il Giornale*, a living legend of Italian journalism, waiting to learn my fate. He stared at my sky-blue down jacket, soaked and puffy, and asked, "Are you going skiing or what?"

No, I wasn't going skiing. I'd simply gotten lost—something that I would continue to do, assiduously, in Milan during my military service (as a member of the air force, but a driver). I'd leave the barracks on Piazza Novelli in my sky-blue uniform, driving a dark blue Fiat 128; and regular as clockwork, I'd get lost every time. Over toward San Siro, around Taliedo, in Lorenteggio, hunting for the road to the military airports of Ghedi (Brescia) or Cameri (Novara). Often driving alone or with one or more officers, once with two pilots of the Frecce Tricolori, the Italian Air Force aerobatic display team. I'd find myself in areas I'd never seen before, in mysterious corners of the city, and I recognized their poetry. Back in civilian dress, now and then, I'd try to find them again. I almost never succeeded. It was as if Milan modestly revealed herself only to provincials in uniform.

In the 1980s I was an occasional guest of friends on Via Grossich (Lambrate district), and then, on my return from London, I rented a place on Via Guicciardini (a cross street of Corso Indipendenza). The first apartment I owned in Milan—on Via Foppa, near Parco Solari—was in 1990: an apartment inherited from an aunt with a terrace facing west. I finally had a point of reference, a home base from which to conduct my explorations. But I almost immediately moved away for work—Moscow, London, and then Washington, DC—and when I came back my Milanese wanderings continued. I didn't mind them, and I don't mind them even now that I know Milan and how to get around it (more or less).

I know that Barona ("Baroness"), in spite of the name, is not an aristocratic part of town; I know that Isola ("Island") is not located in the middle of the sea, and that Inganni ("Deceits") is not a dubious part of town. One Sunday, without a GPS, I made my way to the Cagnola district, an undertaking that still makes me proud. In the past, the district was a country village split up in terms of jurisdiction among the townships of Corpi Santi, Boldinasco, and Villapizzone, names that seem to come straight out of a detective novel by the Ukrainian-born noir author Giorgio Scerbanenco, *The Milanese Kill on Saturdays* (the English rendering of *I milanesi ammazzano al sabato*, 1969). Well, the Cremaschi get lost in Milan every blessed day of the week, I can promise you that.

My outsider status never discouraged me; quite the contrary. I love Milan every bit as much as I love Crema, just in a different way. This is my port of departure; this is the bay that led me out to the greater sea.

I like Milan because it's imperfect—in its urban layout and in its architecture (cities that are too pretty can be boring). I like Milan because it's gray, green, and yellow. I like Milan because it knows how to be paradoxical, like its comedy. I like Milan because it's incurably romantic. I like Milan because it's mysterious, sensual, and political (read *Un amore* [*A Love Affair*, 1963] by Dino Buzzati and *La vita agra* [*It's a Hard Life*, 1962] by Luciano Bianciardi). I like Milan because it's a combination of planning, sheer courage, and random chance; but it's the attitudes of the people who live there that make it special. The Milanese love their city and respect it, unlike the Romans, who all too often just love their city and leave it at that.

And when I write "the Milanese," I'm not just thinking of those who were born here. You can become Milanese, and it can happen in a hurry. Most Milanese come from somewhere else—Crema or Frosinone, Naples or Trieste, Puglia or Sicily, Piedmont or Calabria—and we speak of Milan with gratitude. We're not just paying lip service. If you work in Milan, you know that the city makes no demands: it doesn't shout at you, it makes no claims on you, and that's why we give it as much as we can. During the economic boom of the 1960s, Milan welcomed 650,000 people from all over the country, most from the poorer South of the country. It still welcomes many of us, showing that it's the America of Italy, renewed and reinvented with the assistance of the latest arrivals, in an ongoing palingenesis.

The system of pitching in and helping out lies at the foundation of the city's success. Because it's undeniable. Between 2015 and 2020, before Covid hit, Milan was optimistic and hitting on all cylinders, just as it had been in the 1960s and 1980s: the same eager ambition, the same enduring conviction, the same straightforward enthusiasm. The city will no doubt climb out of the crevasse of the pandemic that opened up beneath it without warning. In fact, the sudden collapse and the array of challenges have allowed Milan to display its seriousness of purpose, the thing that fools can't see—and to avoid, in the future, the dangerous euphoria that seized everyone between 2015 and 2020, when it seemed as if Milan was climbing a stairway to heaven, with apologies to Led Zeppelin. Then, as we all know, the stairway collapsed. Heaven, of course, is still right there.

21. Because Rome is a story unto itself

July 2020, four months into the pandemic. A hot summer afternoon. The streets of Rome were quiet, the piazzas were empty, and many stores had their metal roller blinds shut and fastened. If you kept quiet, you could hear the voices of the fountains. The platoons of Chinese tourists were nowhere to be seen. The American travelers—their hats, their sandals, their cheerful noise—had vanished, as had the pilgrims and their tour buses. Only a few German families challenged the heat that was dripping from the blue sky overhead.

Of Rome's twelve hundred hotels, fewer than two hundred had reopened for business after the first lockdown; some had only five occupied rooms. On Via Veneto—the street of dreams and cinematic history—there were only three hotels in operation. The others were all closed, officially for maintenance.

Out on the streets, you'd run into only a few Italian tourists, looking puzzled. The Romans who weren't at the beaches of Ostia or Fregene went out for an evening stroll; some ventured up to the Gianicolo, the Janiculum Hill, where a cooling west wind brought some relief. Down below, Rome glittered.

It was hard for Italy's capital until mid-2021. The scars are still visible. The tourism industry, which includes hotels, bars, cafés, restaurants, taxis, and museums, is a very substantial part of the Italian economy. It's fundamental for the capital. Rome is a city that's lost its confidence, and it's at risk of grimly resigning itself. That can't be allowed to happen.

Literature is capable of some formidable syntheses. It never announces them, the way that journalism does; it just drops them onto your plate. I happened to read two opinions of Rome, written by two Romans, and they made quite an impression on me.

The first is by a writer and traveler born in the same year as me, Edoardo Albinati, the winner of the 2016 Strega Prize for *La scuola Cattolica* (*The Catholic School*). The insight that so struck me appeared in his next book, *Cuori fanatici* (*Fanatical Hearts*, 2019). In a sort of introduction, separate from the story proper and titled "Prologue to the Southern City," a Roman attempted a general theory of Rome. Who else could dare to try such a thing?

> Skepticism gusts through the city so powerfully that it sweeps away, like so many light reeds, the timid myths, newly blooming: as it corrodes factual reality, it allows countless fanciful variants to sink their roots into its cracks. . . . The city [of Rome] is all one giant scar: seared by sensations so ancient and potent that they must be canceled from memory in order to ensure the survival of those who experience them; it cannot react to the stings of the present day save with a grimace, of helplessness more than any real pain, a leering grin that artists have learned to reproduce all too well.

I found the other insight in a poem by Ugo Reale, who was born in Rome in 1920. A collection of his poetry from 1971, *Un'altra misura* (*Another Measure*), caught my attention during the first lockdown. In it I found this "Lettera a un amico del nord" ("Letter to a Friend from the North"). I thought to myself: *I'd like to have received a letter like this one.* Actually, I guess, I really did receive such a letter, through the strange

meanders of books and words. But it arrived fifty years after
it was sent.

> *I speak to you of the absurd city*
> *that is Rome, with a growing well of anger*
> *because every time I lack*
> *the sheer courage it would take to leave.*
> *Even when your invitation*
> *calls me out at last*
> *I hesitate in a reluctance*
> *that is more than a pretext*
> *or a matter of parallels.*
>
> *For so many years now I've defended*
> *the stones and the red sunsets,*
> *the eternal values, the Latin;*
> *my words died within me*
> *as you laughed while you listened.*
> *But how could I turn my back on*
> *my city, my life?*
> *Abandon the struggle*
> *and that faithful pride?*

Not much has changed for Rome, it would seem. The seventies of the twentieth century and the teens of the twenty-first
century, the temptation of cynicism and the danger of resignation: two sicknesses. But for each there is a treatment.

All intelligent Italians are hoping for the recovery of their
capital; if they don't consider it important, they're not intel-

ligent. Rome is the brightest, most sparkling diamond that we can show off to the world. We can't allow it to be suffocated by incompetence nor to drift into deterioration and decline; nor can we settle for letting it become the virtual playground of international exoticism. "Roman Holiday" is a nice song indeed. But the National, the rock band that sings it, won't clear the garbage away from Rome's streets and piazzas.

The city's decline in recent years has been intolerable, and not only for the Romans. The traditional rivalry with Milan is a relic of the past: I don't know a single Milanese who doesn't wish for the capital's rebirth (and once that happens, okay, it will certainly be fun to rekindle the rivalry). Nowadays the difference between the two cities is stunning. It's not just a question of appearance, cleanliness, and the services provided to the citizens; it's also the mood. Milan is confident (sometimes excessively so); Rome seems to have lost its optimism, even if it suffered less from the pandemic.

How can a city lose its self-respect? It might seem obvious; but you'd have to start with the problems with trash collection, public transportation, the streets, and the parks. In an airy, clean city, where it's easy to get around, it comes naturally to want to roll up your sleeves and get to work. In Rome I have colleagues, friends, in-laws, and three lovely nieces. When the two elder girls come north to Milan, there's no mistaking their relief. A daytime Metro that runs on time and a brightly lit nighttime streetcar can really change your life.

Since 2016, more than 250 buses have caught fire in Rome, inexplicably. Wild boars, rats, seagulls, and even a lonely goat root in uncollected garbage. The city parks are neglected, the streets are full of dangerous potholes. In the spring of 2021, a combination of Covid restrictions and bureaucracy led to a backlog of up to two thousand unburied bodies. A young man

even put up a billboard with these words: MAMMA, I'M SORRY I'VE
NOT BEEN ABLE TO HAVE YOU BURIED YET. Do you know any other
G7 capital city where such things could happen?

Milanese optimism might seem naive—there is no shortage of scandals in the city in the sectors of both health care
and transportation—but Roman cynicism threatens to become
toxic. Solutions? It would be overweening—in fact, ridiculous—
to set them out here. But something could be tried—*must* be
tried.

Why not focus on social streets, for example? They've
worked elsewhere. The goal, I read on socialstreet.it, is "to pro-
mote socializing among neighbors in the same street in order
to build relationships, share necessities, exchange expertise
and knowledge, implement collective projects, and achieve all
the benefits of greater social interaction." Free of charge, it
requires no new websites or platforms: it's based on private
Facebook groups. The first Milanese social street was created
in 2013, following the example set by Bologna. Today there are
more than eighty in Milan, many in the *periferia*, the outskirts
of town. They exist in Rome, too, but are few in number, as are
the people participating.

Is cooperation among residents a minor detail? Certainly;
it would be more important for Rome to build modern waste-
to-energy power plants, which would allow the city to solve
its garbage problem; improve the public transportation; create
bike paths; encourage the presence of traffic police to deal with
the swarms of motorcycles and scooters and prevent parking
violations. Also, to prune the underbrush of political privilege,
behind which the governing class lurks in hiding. But a proliferation of social streets would be a healthy stimulus for the
Campidoglio, the site of Rome's city council, and send a loud
alarm to awaken the slumbering parties, as well as create a

fanfare of optimism. Without optimism, cities freeze up and grind to a halt.

The refrain of "Roman Holiday" says, "Please, think the best of me." So many of us in Italy want to think the best of Rome. But that's not enough. We need Rome to start thinking the best of itself. Then everything will become possible.

22. Because our North and South fight like an old married couple

His last name is Toscani (which means "Tuscans"), he's a Lombard, and he's angered the entire population of the Veneto region: it's a fine geographic mess. Some time ago, during a radio interview, he said, "The Venetians are a tribe of drunkards. Ancestral alcoholics, grandparents, fathers, mothers. . . . Those poor Venetians, it's not their fault. If you were born there, then it's fate. . . . I mean, just listen to their accent: they sound drunk, they sound like alcoholics, a glass of wine, the classic *ombretta*."

Why would Oliviero Toscani, the renowned photographer, ever have said such a thing? He thought he was being funny. "It was an amusing wisecrack. If the only ones who didn't laugh were a few Venetians, then I'm so sorry," he said in self-justification. Amusing? Let's put it this way: the man has a better eye than sense of humor. His lack of success at making a joke is only an aggravating factor. Anyway, there was a storm of objections out of the Veneto region, of course, howls of protest, threats of lawsuits, and political declarations (there's never a shortage of those).

Does that mean it's verboten to make jokes about countries, regions, and cities? Of course not. Does it mean—as the dictatorship of political correctness would have it—that national characteristics are an invention and there are only persons and no such thing as peoples? Again, certainly not. Settings—history, geography, religion (or the lack thereof), culture, economy, food, and cuisine—condition behavior. Every individual is different from every other, but there is an Italian common denominator, just as there are German, French, American, Russian, and Brazilian common denominators. Anyone who denies that has never been to Germany, France, the United States, Russia, or Brazil. Or else they're speaking in bad faith.

There also exist—for basically the same reasons—regional common denominators. Italy has Lombards, Tuscans, and Sicilians. The Lombards tend to be enthusiastic, the Tuscans tend to be tactical, and the Sicilians know how to wait.

Do you like that as a summary? Or is it obvious or corny? Well, whatever you might think of it, I feel pretty certain that none of my readers will take offense: neither in Milan, nor in Florence, nor in Palermo. For one simple reason: I like Lombards, Tuscans, and Sicilians. I like the fact that Italians are different from one another. That fact is unmistakable in the short paragraph I wrote just before. So what am I trying to say here? One simple thing. Or maybe two. Possibly even three.

First: Never tell a joke unless you know you can control it. Irony is the secular sister of mercy; sarcasm is the obnoxious kid brother of intelligence.

Second: An affectionate insight is permissible; a biting generalization is inadvisable. A summation is possible only if you know what you're talking about; otherwise it's just shallow blather.

Third: Never speak nor write about, much less judge, a people publicly, unless you like them and care for them deeply. That's true for Americans, it's true for Europeans, and it's true for other Italians. It's true for everybody.

⁓ঌৄ⁓

This is the main problem underlying many of the quarrels between Italy's North and South, stretching back to the unification of Italy and continuing today. The pandemic has only made matters worse: the lack of understanding among Italy's regions—featuring mayors, governors, commissioners, and citizens—has if anything grown more serious in recent years. There is a lack of empathy, more marked among the ruling class than among the governed, because the authorities tend to emphasize principles, roles, and jurisdictions, underscoring and highlighting differences. We citizens, on the other hand, can try to use our hearts and our memories, allowing us to glimpse more clearly the things that unite us.

A great many mistakes have been made over time. The current yawning gap between North and South—differences in resources, services, and opportunities—is a fault that weighs on all Italians, a stain on our nation. It's one that has engendered hostility, disappointment, and misunderstanding, even though it's obvious that we are one and the same multicolored people.

Outside Italy, from time to time, I've been accused of trying to describe my compatriots without making proper distinctions between North and South ("How can you call a book *La Bella Figura: A Field Guide to the Italian Mind*? Which Italy, which Italians? The Lombards or the Sicilians? The Turinese or the Neapolitans?"). I've always replied: there are shared traits, you just have to look for them. We are a nation held together by television memories and angles of light, large *palazzi* and small streets, dark paintings by luminous artists, naive songs, sun on the beach and soccer on television, wine and oil, pasta and cappuccino, warm welcomes and cold mountain waters. If you can't see that, then too bad for you.

Are there differences between northern and southern Italy? Sure there are, and that's good. But the Italian common denominator exists, and it's not hard to find. If you want to find it, however, you have to look for it. And if you mean to go looking, you have to start with goodwill. Unfortunately, that quality is very scarce these days.

～⋙⋘～

The psychological guerrilla warfare between Italy's North and South is age-old, and it needs to stop. Now, more than ever, we're in desperate need of a truce. Think of the investments that EU aid has finally made possible in transportation, health care, waterworks. Southern Italy could finally glimpse the turning point that we've all been awaiting for far too long.

The most pitiless judgments are always handed down from a distance. As far as that goes, the pandemic has changed very little. Anyone who shares a piece of Italy—places, families, loves, friendships, jobs, experiences—avoids stereotypes because they know how painfully they can wound a person. Young southerners who've studied and who work in northern Italy have brought knowledge and good common sense to the discussion. Northerners who spend time in southern Italy avoid offensive generalizations.

Do you want proof that we're a nation? We Italians, when we meet overseas, recognize each other instantly. We understand what unites us, and we ignore what divides us. Unlike other nationalities, we delight in one another's company. Emilians and Sicilians, Piedmontese and Pugliesi, Romans and Triestines: when we're far away from Italy, we're certain that we're Italians. It's not the product of rational thought; our instincts tell us so.

And the Italians' instincts are rarely wrong.

23. Because Sardinia smells like patience

When the ferryboat from Genoa approached Sardinia at the end of night, we tried to pick up the smell—eucalyptus and helichrysum, grass and sand, warm wind and damp rocks. Most important was not to be noticed. When you're eighteen, you may swear and scream, but you're not supposed to enjoy the poetry of the dawn on the sea. Jealous of our secret, we stood on the deck, watching the coast of the island taking shape, the stale reek of the ship replaced by the fragrance of the land.

That was the 1970s. For many years to come, we traveled to Sardinia in much the same way. We drove an overloaded Vespa on *strade statali*, we caught an overnight ferry from Genoa to Olbia, we spent the night tucked into a sleeping bag outdoors, watching the stars, or inside, in the cafeteria, where large Sardinian families played cards just inches from our feet. We kept on traveling like that even when we could afford better accommodations. It was a ritual filled with a secret euphoria. It was the beginning of discomfort, the beginning of our freedom.

I've been going back to Sardinia for nearly fifty years now, in every season of the year, on practically any pretext that presents itself (holidays, friends, journalism, books, television, theater). I love the place. Sardinia is the oldest part of a very old country, the part of Italy where people live longest and talk least. Sardinia is Italy's western balcony, the place where we sit to calm our anxieties. The interior is beautiful and rugged, the coastline is breathtaking. Fly to Olbia, drive to Santa Teresa Gallura, forty-five miles away, on the northeastern corner of the island. Then follow the coast road southwest for ten miles. You'll see a brown sign: MONTI RUSSU. Not a building in sight, just miles of pine trees, eucalyptus, empty sand beaches, and green water. I've never seen anything like it anywhere else in Europe.

Yes, Sardinia is amazing. Yet it is fragile and vulnerable. The island's coastline extends for 1,150 miles, longer than that of any other region of Italy. A third of the distance is made up of beaches. A hundred years ago, they were inhospitable and malaria ridden; today, they're lovely and welcoming, a gift of nature, a result of history (successive reclamation projects), a demographic corollary (Sardinian's population is one-third that of Sicily). But also the result of a good law. The Piano Paesaggistico Regionale—also known as the Coast Guard Law—prohibits building on the strip of coast extending three hundred meters inland. It has protected a very beautiful part of the world. Every so often, the regional governments try to interfere with it. A very bad idea.

The island's coastline is an immense treasure; if it were to be ruined, as has happened in other Italian regions, the damage would be irreparable. There are roughly 270,000 second homes in Sardinia, empty ten months out of every year: that's more than enough. The greedy land grabbers are almost always from the mainland peninsula or foreigners. The benefits for the people of Sardinia of new construction for tourists would be modest at best (a few building contracts at the very beginning; a few seasonal jobs to manage them). Seriously, should they sell the family jewels for such a pittance?

Italian beaches are a stage, every one of them. They offer settings, plot twists, dialogue, food for thought, surprises, cunning moves, colors, and uproar. Until about twenty years ago, sociologists, humorists, and journalists dug eagerly into this magnificent treasury of human material. These days it's less common, and that's a pity. There's so much to think about when sitting on the sand of Rena Majore Beach, township of Aglientu, in Gallura, with Corsica in your eyes and the mistral wind in your hair. For example: Why doesn't anyone go swimming? City pools are packed, young Italian swimmers are victorious in competitions across Europe, but when it comes to the sea, people of all ages limit themselves to chatting and floating. If they do swim, they stop after five or so strokes. Sooner or later you're likely to encounter the same people running, panting and exhausted, in the hot sunlight, trying to stay in shape.

Second baffling question: What's become of topless sunbathers? Has a fear of sunlight spread, or has our sense of modesty been recalibrated? Has there been some change in the law, have fashions changed, or is there something different in the way we look at things? I've been coming here since the long-ago year of 1973. I remember what these beaches looked like in the 1970s and early '80s: you were more likely to run into a talking sea bass than a bikini top. Nowadays, sex is a public matter: fodder for social media, an entrée on television with a side dish of commercials. But women's breasts have gone back to being intensely private.

~~~

It's called Cala Grande, or "big cove," but it's better known as Valle della Luna, "valley of the moon." It's at the far tip of Capo Testa, which in turn lies at the very end of Santa Teresa Gallura, which occupies the northernmost tip of Sardinia. It's a spectacular place: a perfect combination of green and light blue, white and gray, water and mastic trees, sky and granite. Sea daffodils grow everywhere, and the air is redolent with the scent of the everlasting plant.

Valle della Luna attracts painters, poets, nudists, and musicians, flower children and cops who are there to keep an eye on the flower children. I discovered it in the mid-'70s, and I came back often to engage in activities such as scuba diving, lovemaking, field trips, and reporting. The place has managed to survive because it's hard to reach; if it's become well known, outside of Italy as well, that's thanks to—or perhaps the fault of—the hippie community. The locals have tried to discourage them, evict them, or relocate them: all efforts have proved futile. The Valle della Luna hippies are authentic and locally brewed. They come here, they play music and sing, they smoke whatever it is they're inclined to smoke, they eat whatever they can lay their hands on, and they sleep pretty much where they lie down. They don't take it wrong if the other vacationers look at them as if they're some exotic species: if anything, they might approach them to try to sell them a bracelet.

I remember the opening act of a musical festival. Spread out over the sandy slope rolling down to the sea was a national miscellany: aging longhairs and lawyers at the end of their summer vacations, enthusiastic young girls wearing the wrong shoes, older beachgoers covered with tattoos and forty-year-olds with lumbago, euphoric thirty-year-olds and insurance adjusters with their families. It was an Italy that was getting along fine amid a babel of regional accents; and when they all left, there wasn't so much as a scrap of paper on the ground or the echo of a quarrel in the air—a lovely picture to carry in your mind's eye while returning to the mainland in the advancing fall, when we could all go back to arguing with one another.

24. Because wine is a sentimental education, and espresso is a truce

I've written little, if anything, about wine. I talk about it only rarely. But I drink it with meals. Every single meal, without exception. Stew accompanied by orangeade is, quite simply, against my religion. My father, who lived to nearly a hundred, insisted that water with meals created internal rust. He drank water at the end of a meal and plenty more throughout the course of the day. But at lunch or dinner, he had a glass of wine. My son, age twenty-nine, offers the people who dine in his restaurant, Sarius al Lago, near Crema, good wine at reasonable prices: he spends a fair amount of time choosing just the right one, and he insists that his guests appreciate the effort. That includes diners his age, whether they're couples out for dinner or larger groups.

It's not just a family attitude; it's also a source of national pride.

When I'm in the United States, I always order a glass of wine with lunch, especially business lunches: I make it a point of pride. I love to see the look of concern in the eyes of my fellow diners. Their embarrassed silence seems to hiss *You're an alcoholic!* At that point, pausing to build the drama, I prepare my theatrical declaration. "Ladies and gentlemen!" I declaim. "Who of you is going to down a martini this evening? Followed by another and then—why not?—a third martini never hurt anybody, right? Who are we going to have to drive home after dinner, because they can barely stand up? Who's going to head back to the hotel and then start hitting the minibar? Is that likely to be an Italian or an American? Will it be me or one of you?" At that point, the whole table falls silent. Here and there, other people at the table will order a glass of wine, with a smile and a look of gratitude in their eyes.

Okay, it's a cheap victory. But it's worth pointing out Italy's superiority on this subject from time to time. There is no such thing as a world wine championship season, there's just a final playoff, and the contenders are always the same: Italy versus France. The Italians and the French understand wine, even if they know nothing about it and never drink it. It's an expertise that lurks in our traditions, our proverbs, our memories, and our conversations. We Italians understand wine spontaneously, and we have since we were children. We might say that we drink it with our mother's milk if it weren't for the fact that once upon a time, in the Italian countryside, that actually was the case, and even for us that's excessive.

The fact that we never demonized wine but instead transformed it into a moment for the family and for socializing has been by far the most powerful weapon against the alcoholic drift of the newer generations. In Anglo-Saxon and northern European societies, the implacable thirst for alcoholic beverages that begins the minute young people reach the legal age—and of course, even before that—must be linked to prohibitions and restrictions. I feel sure of that. In Italy, too, unfortunately, there are plenty of people who overdo it, and that's been the case for a while now. But it's hard liquor, more than wine, that causes the greatest personal and social harm.

In Italy, drunkenness is not yet a point of pride, as it is elsewhere. It's been that way for many years. My great-grandfather Francesco, a farmer, wanted to be able to hold his head up among his friends who had plenty of titles and honorifics to append to their names ("Dott." for *Dottore*, "Prof." for *Professore*, "Cav."

for *Cavaliere*, "Comm." for *Commendatore*). He therefore had the following printed on his calling card: *Francesco Severgnini, Bev.* "Bev." was meant to stand for *Bevitore*, literally "drinker": a man who could hold his wine and knew when to stop. A man who knew how to drink, in other words.

There is no other country on Earth where every region grows wine grapes. But that's how it is in Italy. From Piedmont to Sicily, from Puglia to Friuli–Venezia Giulia, from Lombardy to Sardinia, and from Tuscany to Campania, wine is everywhere, and it's good wherever you find it. Sometimes it's memorable. We don't just know how to drink it; we try to understand it, each of us with our own knowledge and family background. But we're nearly all able to distinguish a good wine from a bad one, the right temperature from the wrong one, a fragrant bouquet from a disagreeable odor.

The comment "It tastes slightly of cork," when uttered with some embarrassment in the presence of a silent waiter, is less laughable than it might at first seem. I've had numerous experiences with that taste while traveling around the world. Many foreigners, including those who are willing to spend a lot of money for a bottle, don't even notice that their wine tastes of cork. That's for one simple reason: they don't love wine. They just buy it and drink it.

I guess you've noticed it while visiting Italy. The company at dinner is numerous, noisy, convivial, thirsty, and ravenous. The men shout out jokes, convinced that they're being funny. The women all laugh, convinced that the men are being ridiculous. At the head of the table, beaming, sits an Italian signore, well along in years, who exclaims, *"Pago io!"* In Italian, he's claiming the right to pay, urging the waiter to bring him the check. Everyone else is no doubt thinking inwardly, "Fine!" while they shout out, "No! You're too kind!"

The occasion is festive and cheerful, the wine has done its job, the banqueters are all in a fine mood. This is a moment all restaurateurs cherish, because no one looks at the prices on the menu. And so the waiter comes over to the table and politely inquires, "Would you care to see the dessert menu?" The whole room holds its collective breath. The evening's grand finale, and a substantial portion of the check, depend upon a single phrase: "Oh, I'll just have an espresso."

If anyone at the table utters those words, it's over. Everyone else will fall into line like ducks on a lake. "Oh, sure, I'll have the same." "Espresso for us, too." "Sounds good, a nice short espresso is just the thing." Mr. Let-me-pay!, though eager to amplify the grandeur of his sacrifice, declares, "So that makes ten espressos. And please bring the check to me." The waiter glares with distaste at the young lady who was first to utter the fateful words "Oh, I'll just have an espresso." If he could, he'd stride straight into the kitchen, come back with a crock of hot fudge, and pour it down her neckline.

This, however, is an exception. On the whole, espresso doesn't divide Italians. If anything, it unites them. It's a liquid pause in the day, brimming over with consequences, a black beverage with a clear significance. "Shall we get an espresso?" marks the beginning of friendships, love stories, negotiations, projects, and contracts (or perhaps the dissolution of the same). The correct translation of "Let's get an espresso" is "I want to talk to you. But I can't do it on the street; I don't want to do it at a desk; I'm not asking you to come to my house. I don't even want to talk while sitting down, like Americans, Austrians, or Australians. No, I want to drink an espresso standing up."

Whether it's from a proper café or an office espresso machine makes no real difference. An Italian *caffè* is neither an appointment nor an obligation. It's a treaty negotiation; sometimes it's a cease-fire. Most important is that nobody has the feeling that they're too exposed or suspects that they've gone too far.

25. Because we instinctively know what's good and genuine

Immediately after the first lockdown in 2020, an Italian brand of coffee filled the plate glass windows of Italy's cafés with signs that proclaimed: KEEPING OUR PROPER DISTANCE, BUT UNITED IN FLAVOR. Let's admit that of the two statements in that slogan, the second is more persuasive and much easier to check.

Physical distancing—which, for some unknown reason, we call "social distancing"—ought to be a fleeting phenomenon and has given rise to numerous interpretations. Our national unity in matters of taste, on the other hand, is unquestionable. There are certain individual and geographic differences, but the culinary and nutritional expertise of the Italians can be observed at all levels of education and income. No other country on Earth can boast the same variety and high quality of raw materials, the same sheer imagination in cooking, equal levels of widespread knowledgeability. An Italian never just *thinks* that a dish is tasty or that a bowl of pasta has been cooked just right. They *know* it.

Anyone harboring lingering doubts should have visited Milan during Expo 2015. The theme was "Feeding the Planet." Between May 1 and October 31, the city welcomed twenty-two million visitors, a third of whom were not Italian. Why are we Italians so very good when it comes to our skills in cooking and our preferences in dining? Many have asked me this question, so I've come up with a concise answer. What's the secret of Italian food? The five *F*'s: *family, feuds, fantasy, feelings,* and *fashion.*

Let's start with family. The worldwide popularity of Italian cuisine dates back to the turn of the twentieth century, when Italians emigrated en masse to northern Europe, the United States, and South America. Some started inns and trattorias in their new cities to offer their fellow immigrants the only kind of cooking they knew: home cooking. Immigrants from other nations soon recognized that they could eat well by frequenting Italian establishments; they came in droves, and word spread. Before many decades passed, that reputation had spread around the world.

The home has always been, for us Italians, a culinary workshop that has combined simplicity, quality, and common sense. Of course, in the great courts of the Renaissance, food was superb and sophisticated, but it was consumed only by a very small number of individuals, and in fact, that school of cooking has by and large been forgotten. Traditional Italian cuisine—the cooking that has won international supremacy—is, on the other hand, the product of a community, based on skills and expertise that are shared and handed down. It is a popular art form that rises from the bottom up, one that everyone is capable of appreciating.

French cuisine, outstanding though it might be, was handed down from on high. When in the sixteenth century the Florentine noblewoman Catherine de' Medici married Henri II, who would one day become king of France, and in time became the queen mother of three other sovereigns (François II, Charles IX, and Henri III), she taught the French court how to cook (so the Italian legend goes, at least!). That marked the birth of transalpine culinary excellence (in Italy, we refer to France as "beyond the Alps"): it has always been a magnificent aristocratic product, and it has never really changed its basic nature. "Of all the arts practiced in France, the art of cooking is the least rooted in daily life, the only one, you might say, that demands the hand of a professional," wrote the future Nobel laureate Eugenio Montale in 1953. Almost seventy years later, most Italians share this admiring yet cautious view.

And now we come to the second cause of the excellence of Italian cuisine. Public life in Italy is based on feuding. Centuries of foreign domination have forced the Italians to seek comfort, security, and a sense of identity in their own communities. And a community can *also*—I was about to write *above all*—find its identity in food. Every region, province, and township in Italy has at least one culinary specialty, one recipe or preparation in which it considers itself unrivaled. An American might discern no difference between the tortellini of Bologna and those of Modena. The Bolognese and the Modenese, however, would beg to differ. The citizens of both cities feel they're the unquestioned masters of their culinary technique (and they're both wrong, the townspeople of Castelfranco Emilia would patiently explain; in fact, the town built a monument shaped like a belly button in honor of the local tortellino). And as long as we're on the subject: Crema's *tortello dolce* (filled with raisins, nutmeg, and amaretto) is far and away superior to the *tortello di zucca* of Mantua (with pumpkin filling—delicious but predictable).

These differences engender something more than mere competition; they produce a spectacular variety, a rich array of rivalries. Italy's temperate climate, from the Dolomites to the islands south of Sicily, provides sublime raw materials to work with. Working since 1986, the Slow Food movement has identified five hundred presidia featuring thirteen thousand producers; it has highlighted and popularized territories and processing techniques; and it has rescued from imminent extinction heirloom breeds and varieties of vegetables and fruit from onions and garlic to artichokes and apricots. The Slow Food association has expanded from Italy to 150 countries around the world.

And then there's fantasy—imagination—a very important factor. The Italians may not be the largest food producers on Earth, but they are unbeatable when it comes to adaptation. Paolo Marchi, a tireless veteran gastronome and food critic as well as the mastermind behind the Identità Golose festival, puts it this way: "The Chinese have developed forty thousand recipes, we Italians have maybe produced two thousand. They invented spaghetti independently, as we well know. But the idea that you shouldn't overcook spaghetti—the concept of 'al dente'—that's Italian. The world likes to chew." What about the tomato? Imported from America, it bided its time as a strictly ornamental plant for centuries until the Italians turned it into their signature ingredient. And coffee? It grows in Africa, Latin America, and Asia, and it was first brought to Venice by the Turks. But it is Italian espresso that has conquered the world. In the port of Trieste, coffee arrives from twenty different countries; it is then shipped back out to 140 countries around the planet.

The fourth element: feelings. Food is nutrition, but it's also emotion, and when it comes to feelings, we Italians are professionals in the field. For starters, we like to spend time together, and restaurants are convivial theaters of togetherness. But then, Italian chefs are also, almost invariably, extremely sentimental. Throughout the rest of Europe, there are plenty of excellent chefs and restaurants; all too often, however, they slip into the traps of virtuosity, competition, and mere exhibitionism (Gordon Ramsay is a good example of this). Certainly, even Italian chefs have allowed themselves to be tempted by television and celebrity status; but nearly all, whether famous, well known, or lesser known, have been able to preserve their passion for their craft and their empathy for their guests and diners. Listening to a young chef describe his *risotto alle erbe* or his beef *brasato* is magical. He seems to be sharing a secret.

The fifth element: fashion. Italian cuisine is not a fleeting fad intended for the elite, with special techniques strictly for initiates. Nouvelle cuisine is passé; molecular cuisine, too, will soon be in our rearview mirrors. Spaghetti, risotto, lasagna, pizza, polenta, mozzarella, Parmesan, prosciutto, and gelato—these are the past, the present, and the future, global words that the world loves to hear and repeat. The fundamentals of our cuisine—fresh products, simple preparations, short cooking times, and just a few flavorings—have influenced the world's eating habits. Hundreds of millions of families around the world have incorporated them into their daily diet.

The international restaurant business has figured this out, too, and for years it has been on the same wavelength. Anyone who travels much is well aware that many major hotels have at least two restaurants. One is silent and elegant and has a name such as Chez Gustave or Bistrot La Tour; the other is more brightly lit and less expensive and is called L'Olivo—the Olive Tree—or something like that. Take a close look next time: L'Olivo is much more popular than Chez Gustave. And that's worth any number of gold medals.

26. Because many criticize us, but nearly everyone copies us

I have always wondered what it is about us Italians that so captivates foreigners. This isn't a fable that we tell to console ourselves; it's true. I've observed this attraction at work all over the world. Italy enjoys a special indulgence afforded no other nation on Earth.

One explanation is geopolitical. We stopped being conquerors 1,700 years ago, if, that is, we wish to include the Roman emperors among our ancestors. As soon as we tried our hand at it again, we piled up a collection of disasters. The dream of African empire embraced first by Prime Minister Giovanni Giolitti and later by Mussolini failed miserably. We Italians have, sadly, committed our share of atrocities, and this must not be forgiven nor forgotten. But we've always been amateur imperialists: our limited attention span as conquistadors has lightened our guilt and helped our reputation.

Another possible explanation is demographic. Over the past 150 years, Italy has filled the world with emigrants, around thirty-five million of them, ranging from the Venetian peasants who set out for Brazil all the way up to researchers following the siren song of opportunities in Boston or California. They have been hard workers, sociable and convivial, open to new ideas. Maybe not always; occasionally these qualities developed in a younger generation. But once our emigrants emerge from their shell, they tend to participate. In the twentieth century, this has been the case in Germany, Switzerland, France, Belgium, Australia, South America, Canada, and the United

States. Today, twenty million US citizens claim Italian ancestry. The list of Italian American politicians, actors, directors, singers, and scientists is virtually endless, from Frank Sinatra, Francis Ford Coppola, and Lady Gaga to Nancy Pelosi, Robert De Niro, and the immunologist Anthony Fauci, who kept President Trump from making things even worse.

Still, these considerations are not enough to explain the persistent allure we seem to exert on the peoples of other countries. There is, however, another explanation, which may prove more persuasive. The idea of Italy is bound up with pleasant concepts: art, landscape, quiet waters, fine food and wine, movies, music, fashion, and design. Sometimes these connections slip into the realm of the stereotype, encouraged by the low-effort promotion of tourism undertaken by so many Italian government agencies. International public opinion isn't particularly sophisticated, and admiration and condemnation are frequently superficial. Still, we tend to emerge pretty well (except perhaps for our politics) from this global court of judgment, overarching and hasty though it may be. So we have no reason to complain.

In my books and in many articles, I have done my best to delve into the reasons for this fascination. I've come to a conclusion: the *dolce vita* endures, but it is no longer a cinematic reference. Nor is it a caricature bound up with tourism. No, it's an evocative image, an abiding temptation, and a reliable consolation. We Italians feel obliged to wage constant combat against the dictatorship of the picturesque, but we can hardly deny that Italy provides many people around the world the sensual and psychological comfort that they seek—perhaps from a safe distance.

By trusting in their intuition and employing a healthy dose of patience, nations can listen to and learn from each other, almost as if they were so many songs. No other country is our equal when it comes to the difficult things (family ties, food, and art), and none is so deplorably sloppy when it comes to the easy things (respecting rules, mostly). Our finer national qualities are the (inimitable) product of centuries of history; our shortcomings are the (irritating) result of civic laziness. Therefore, Italy is a place that can drive a person into a seething rage or a delighted state of ecstasy in the space of a mere hundred yards and the arc of no more than ten minutes. But Italy is also capable of charming and fascinating the world, which just doesn't seem able to forget us.

Our national genius is no longer that of Leonardo da Vinci or even the genius—less impressive, perhaps, but nevertheless delicious—of those who come up with exquisite culinary creations, handsome clothing, and eye-catching objects (in the United States, chairs and shoes are expected to be comfortable; in Italy, sexy). Our genius can be seen in our everyday behavior.

It would be nonsensical to describe the recent Covid pandemic as a romantic experience, much less to claim that everyone who worked on the front line—physicians, nurses, health care workers—would gladly sign up for the same experience a second time. But let's say it clearly: the Italians, compared to other nations, showed composure, strength, and resourcefulness. The psychological consequences of isolation, for such an extroverted nation, might easily have been far more serious. The collection of sixty million individual cases that we call Italy acquitted itself quite well. That may be because feeling like a unique, individual case, in certain situations, can bolster your self-respect and make it easier to react.

"Who else is as good at turning a crisis into a party?" an English friend of mine asked me when she heard how Italy was responding to the lockdowns. My answer was: It wasn't a party, it was a test of strength. An exhausting ordeal. So true is this that in the immediate aftermath, the classic set of shortcomings promptly emerged: delays in vaccinations, sloppiness, lots of official statements, and very few crucial details; far too many complaints and the usual protests; a profusion of cunning maneuvers, masquerading as noble defenses of sacred rights.

Still, it's true: when faced with the virus, we acquitted ourselves well. And we surprised the world. Not as much as we surprised ourselves, of course.

27. Because we want to work from home, but we enjoy being together

INPS, Italy's national public retirement agency, recently suffered a number of cyberattacks. The agency itself admitted that that was the case and informed its users that it had "promptly notified the Italian Data Protection Authority of the data breach." It used the term *data breach* in English. And any Italian reader might respond: "Well, that's technically correct." Italian even has a word, *breccia*, that resembles the English "breach" and indeed means an intrusion, a violation, or an unauthorized entry. But the crucial question is: How many Italians are familiar with the term *data breach*? Why make use of cryptic English vocabulary to communicate with millions of ordinary Italians in times like this?

Italy's Accademia della Crusca, the world's oldest linguistic academy and the most respected research body for the study of the Italian language, asked the same question. Of course, there are far more pressing matters these days in Italy; the Accademia della Crusca knows it, we who put out books and newspapers know it, and so do our buyers and readers. But the words we use are still important. And in times like these, more than ever.

The pointless use of an Anglicism in current Italian is more than just clumsy; it makes it harder for readers to understand, and it tends to put up barriers, especially for those who are in the greatest need of protection and information. Just think of an elderly person, living alone, who speaks no English and spends little or no time on the internet: that person is physiologically, psychologically, and technologically vulnerable. Why undermine them with the dictionary as well? It's possible—indeed, quite likely—that the person in question will fail to understand certain expressions and will moreover have neither the interest nor the resources to find out more.

Now, admittedly, the term *data breach* applies to a specific case. Furthermore, *FaceTime, Teams, Zoom,* and *webinar* are English terms that do apply in specific situations, such as meetings and distance learning. But let's take an English word such as *droplet.* Was there some reason that the perfectly adequate Italian diminutive, *gocciolina,* which also describes the main vector of Covid infection, shouldn't have been used? Was it too adorable? Whatever shortcomings it may or may not have had, it had one clear advantage: everyone reading Italian would understand it, whatever their age, level of education, or walk of life.

Now, it's true that during the pandemic, we Italians almost immediately abandoned the use of *swab* and went back to the solid Italian term *tampone,* but we still use *dispenser* to refer to a *distributore di liquido disinfettante*—a liquid disinfectant dispenser. The term *drive-through* has been coopted directly from the world of car washes to the domain of blood tests and vaccinations. It is no doubt praiseworthy that the new contact-tracing app should be called Immuni, in clear Italian. Had it worked, we would have been even happier.

Anglicisms in the time of coronavirus are surprising even when we move away from the area of health care. Such imported words as *lo sharing*—for the Italian *condivisione*—don't really pose that much of a problem: the new term was introduced along with the new services themselves, and anyone who uses them is sure to know them. But how many Italians, among those who couldn't leave home to do their shopping due to advanced age, reasonable caution, or health considerations, understood that concealed behind the baffling English phrase *food delivery* lurked the good old familiar Italian phrase *consegna a domicilio*? How many parents would have liked to help their children with *l'e-learning* but barely knew what that was?

We've left for last the words most emblematic of the times we're living in. Why use *lockdown* and *smart working* in Italian? You may well reply: Well, by now everybody understands them! Not so: a great many do, but not everybody. There are plenty of perfectly good Italian equivalents of *lockdown*: *blocco, chiusura, isolamento, reclusione.* Yet we've all surrendered to the new terms, and this author is no exception. I say, and I write, *lockdown.* It has become an Italian word for all intents and purposes. Perhaps this new and global word is used to describe a new and global phenomenon—and, to a certain extent, to exorcise it. *"Dove hai trascorso il lockdown?"* ("Where did you spend your lockdown?") seems less stark and disturbing than *"Dove sei rimasto recluso?"* ("Where were you incarcerated?").

And then there's *il lavoro da casa*, or *telelavoro*—in English, "remote work" or "working from home." But we Italians also call it *smart working*, and we can add it to our linguistic inventions (among them *Autogrill* for motorway restaurant, *autostop* for hitchhiking, *camping* for campsite, *smoking* for tuxedo, *spider* for convertible, *spot* for commercial). We're a people of imagination.

To start with: to call it *smart working—lavoro intelligente*, or intelligent labor—would seem to imply that working in an office is a stupid way to work—which may sometimes be true but quite often is not. Working in the company of other people, in fact, is not merely comforting, it can also be useful. There's such a thing as collective intelligence; it's found in cities, places, and groups. But that ship has sailed. Let there be *smart working*. But let's try to do it with some common sense.

First question: Is it good or bad? Answer: it's good. In a few months' time, we made a giant leap forward that might have taken years under normal conditions. Any individual organization—and the government—would have found some excuse for delaying. The virus put our backs against the wall—a position in which we Italians traditionally do our best work. But let's not overlook a series of potential pitfalls.

1. *Prolonged isolation:* We've experienced it, and it's not healthy.

2. *A lack of elasticity:* Excessive control on the employer's part (technology is an enabler of this).

3. *Too much elasticity:* The absence of clearly defined working hours. There are workers who start their day on WhatsApp at 7:00 a.m. and end it on Zoom at 11:00 p.m.

4. *Unfair working conditions:* It's hard to work from home in crowded, cramped spaces with an old laptop and a bad connection. Don't forget: six million Italian families, a quarter of the population, don't even use the internet.

5. *Salaries at risk:* Companies save money through smart working (on transportation expenses, company

cafeterias, heating, air-conditioning, real estate, rent), but there are employers who are already considering cutting wages for those who work from home.

6. *Risks for women:* Child care and housework, in Italy, fall to them above all. Smart working can't become housework squared. Otherwise, it's three cheers for the office and the commuter's life! At least you get to catch your breath for a few hours each day.

In more introverted nations, being under a sort of house arrest isn't such a traumatic experience. Ignoring people from home, as opposed to ignoring them in the office, is a relatively minor hardship. But in Italy, a highly sociable society, spending time with other human beings is considered to be not a source of annoyance but rather an opportunity and frequently a pleasure—a chance to look at other people, study other people, chat, or sit quietly but companionably; to consult and be consulted; to take part in meetings and then complain about the meetings; to exchange ideas, photocopies, sighs, and tokens for the coffee vending machine; to feel a little less alone.

For some Italians, therefore, smart working doesn't look all that smart. There are already some who consider it to be a postmodern form of confinement. Staying home by choice is one thing; doing it obligatorily is quite another. To make light of it, we would venture to adapt Article 284 of the Italian Code of Criminal Procedure by replacing a few words: *house arrest* with *smart working*, *judge* with *employer*, *person harmed* with *company*, and *defendant* with *employee*. The result is as follows:

1. With the order requiring smart working, the employer instructs the employee not to leave his home or other place of private residence, or else a public place of care or assistance, or else, here established, from a sheltered group home.

    1-b. The employer has established a place of smart working in order to ensure in any case the company's privileged demands for guardianship and protection.

    1-c. The cautionary measure of smart working cannot be served in an illegally occupied building.

2. When necessary, the employer will impose limits or prohibitions upon the employee's ability to communicate with people other than those who cohabit with and assist him.

3. If the employee cannot otherwise provide for his indispensable needs for ordinary existence or if he begins to slip into a situation of absolute poverty, the employer can authorize him to absent himself during the day from his place of smart working, but only for the amount of time strictly necessary to provide for the previously mentioned needs or else to carry out another type of gainful employment.

Buon lavoro! Enjoy your workday!

28. Because we know the line that separates the courteous from the intrusive

Can a man hold a door open for a woman? That question was posed by *The Lily*, a publication targeting millennial women and an offshoot of the *Washington Post*. I can assure my young female readers that this debate is not a new one; it's at least a quarter century old. I recall the episode—in Washington, DC, in fact—in the springtime of 1995: as I was entering a restaurant, I held the door open for a woman. She turned around and spat, "I can manage." Since then, whenever I'm in the United States, I tend to avoid acts of gallantry. You never know.

Let me be clear: #MeToo is an absolutely justified and admirable protest movement. For centuries, women have put up with sexual insults, abuses, and harassment, and not only in the United States. The predatory instincts of many males have found a perfect hunting ground in the workplace. In movies, music, politics, and various other fields, until just a few years ago, the bed or the couch has been a threatening presence for any woman with a job or a profession. In many countries and many lines of work, this still holds true, it's sad to say. Many women—in Italy, too—are forced to submit to gazes, comments, and humiliations that no man will ever experience.

All the same, I am forced to ask: Aren't we overdoing it?

This is a question and a concern that could be misread and misused, but let me rely on the instincts and understanding of my female readers. We have had this discussion frequently, I recall, in the editorial offices of the *Corriere della Sera*'s weekly magazine *7*, staffed by young and largely female journalists.

I've heard a variety of differing opinions, but I've had confirmation of something I'd already guessed: intelligent women understand just how sensitive and complicated the issues are. Italian men know the boundary between courtesy and stepping over lines, between courtship and oppression; but some decide to ignore that boundary. That is intolerable. But courtesy and courtship are a part of life—even in the workplace.

Do you remember McCarthyism? It was a collective hysteria that, in the name of anticommunism, spread injustice and suffering throughout the United States in the early 1950s. (It took its name from Republican senator Joseph McCarthy, the paladin of that demented crusade.) The term survives, and it's come to designate an atmosphere of diffuse and general suspicion in which it becomes impossible to defend yourself. Well, let's try to keep that from happening in Italy. Sexual predators and harassers—who, unfortunately, let me reiterate the point, exist in Italy as well—hope for nothing better: if everyone's guilty, then no one's guilty! Instead, the guilt is blazingly clear, and so is the innocence—as long as you look at the world with clear, clean eyes.

I remember in 2006, before I started my summer teaching stint at Middlebury—a college in Vermont that specializes in teaching foreign languages—I was given a stack of paper. It included guidelines on how to behave with students, among other instructions: hands and how important it was not to place them on shoulders, doors and the urgency of leaving them open, attitudes to avoid, questions not to ask, answers not to give. I also remember one trifling incident. One morning, a particularly gifted student turned in a disappointing assignment. I asked her, with a laugh, whether she'd been out partying or simply hadn't gotten enough sleep. What was I thinking when I made *that* joke? The young woman complained to the department chair, claiming that my comment in class had profoundly upset her.

Since then, everywhere you turn, things have only gotten worse. I've been to US colleges and universities several times since, and I realize that the professors are walking on eggshells: the risk of being misunderstood is elevated, the potential consequences are grave. All it takes is an unfortunate turn of phrase, an adjective, a gesture, an offhand reference. I met an Italian professor who has been working for years with American university students: undergraduates, the younger ones. He told me that introductions have become a veritable minefield. After asking "What's your name?" and being told "George" or "Caroline," one is then expected to ask, "And what are your pronouns?" If George replies, "He, him, his," that means that George identifies as male. If George replies, "She, her, hers," it means that George identifies as female. If George replies, "They, them, theirs," then George identifies as gender fluid. The same, of course, goes for Caroline.

I'm not going to provide name, location, or institution lest I expose the professor to reprisals. I will just add that other eyewitness accounts confirm that teaching in US educational institutions has become a veritable obstacle course. The risk of a professional censure is real and imminent. One way of avoiding trouble, I've been told, is to follow this handy rule of thumb: "Validate, do not contextualize." Because ignoring context—gender, ethnic background, social class, opinions, situations—is risky.

The newly intolerant are at risk of triggering an outbreak of old intolerance; it wouldn't be the first time. This is a lesson we should learn, even in Italy. So should women, even young women and people of color. It's true: they've had to put up with the intolerable, and it is only right that they have reacted and are now demanding respect. The movements—#MeToo, Black Lives Matter—are not only eminently worthy of support; they were also inevitable. Hypocritical and racist men conceal fangs behind their smiles, but some have been caught red-handed, and the attitudes of many others have changed. The credit for this goes to women, young people, honest minds. But let's not overdo it: indignation is just a step short of fanaticism, and it's never worth crossing that line.

But we also run a few risks when it comes to the environmental issue. There's no doubt that if the world has awakened to the danger, credit must go to the young and the very young. *Sustainability* was becoming nothing more than a rote term for politicians, corporations, and conference attendees. The climate—in spite of all we've seen and suffered—was starting to seem like a tired old topic. Then came Greta the Menace (and I intend that as a compliment), protest marches, school strikes, and #FridaysForFuture, and they managed to involve three different generations in the issue. But let's not forget, before it's too late: there's a difference between an honest reaction and full-blown aggression. Certain excesses of zeal—certain harsh stances palmed off as honest purity—are certain to make things worse: for the environment, for young people, for women, and for the most vulnerable ethnic groups. We certainly need respect and understanding, and even severity when called for. But the Red Guards, the Thought Police, are insidious threats and, over the long run, are counterproductive.

Every action, in fact, provokes a reaction. Certain polemical excesses—linguistic correctness taken to the verge of hysteria, intransigence that metastasizes into contempt, severity that becomes cruelty, history derided and statues knocked down like tenpins—threaten to benefit the very worst aspects of the far Right everywhere. Is that what the new generations want? A world of protest marches in which other people make the decisions? I don't think so. We all need help: even women, even young people, even people of color. If these categories manage to alienate the moderates to the point of pushing them into the opposite camp, that would be a problem for everyone.

Comprehension isn't compromise, kindness isn't weakness, savagery isn't strength.

I know very well what the reaction would be if I uttered these words in an English-speaking university classroom (possibly also in an Italian-speaking one!): "Okay, boomer." Are you familiar with the expression? It's a mocking, offhand accusation of paternalism. It's the response, polemical and condescending, that those born at the tail end of the twentieth century and the beginning of the twenty-first century use to dismiss baby boomers like me, born between the mid-1940s and the mid-1960s.

An answer that is satisfying and effective in a slashing fashion spawned on Twitter and TikTok and soon turned into a meme. But it's also a simplistic response, and counterproductive. There are a lot of us boomers, and even if we've gotten a lot wrong, we aren't all evil and selfish. Don't consider us as your fathers, your mothers, and your uncles and aunts, but *do* consider us as your allies. You need allies, because your— our—adversaries are cynical, powerful, and well organized.

Count your cards, youngsters. And then let us know.

29. Because small churches are better than grand defenders of the faith

The phone call came without advance warning: Would I be willing to lead a meeting about Saint Maria Goretti? Her remains were going to be taken back to her birthplace—Corinaldo, in the Marche region—for a week's stay, from January 21 to 28, 2020. I told the caller that I knew too little about her. It's true, I admitted: all too frequently writers and lecturers find themselves traveling the length of Italy to discuss topics they know nothing about, but there can be too much of a good thing. Certainly, I regretted declining the invitation, because it had been extended by the bishop of Senigallia, Franco Manenti, who had been our parish priest as a young man and later became the vicar of Crema Cathedral.

I knew I could offer extenuating circumstances to plead with my spouse, my relatives, and various monsignors, all of whom would be sympathetic and understanding. What I hadn't taken into account, however, was my conscience, which is shrewd and relentless.

I started reading up on Maria Goretti to get a better idea of the opportunity I was renouncing. And I was quickly disabused of my notions, as I realized everything I remembered was vague and mistaken. At the center of the story was a horrible case of domestic femicide; unfortunately, an all-too-modern and relevant topic. The victim was a preteen girl with a troubled and burdensome history: she came from a large family, her father was a farmhand, and they lived in brutal poverty. I had only the laziest and most stereotypical idea of who Maria

Goretti was. When we were kids, if we wanted to describe an exaggeratedly chaste girl our age, we'd say, "Forget about her, she's a *santamariagoretti*"—*Saint Maria Goretti*, all run together, as if to highlight our incurious ignorance.

Maria Goretti was born in 1890, the third of seven children in a family of farmworkers. The Goretti family moved to Lazio province in 1897, into the Agro Pontino, or Pontine Marshes, where European pear trees and fava beans were farmed—a territory of large landowners and plantations, poverty, grueling menial labor, and, of course, malaria, which indeed carried off the father almost immediately. Marietta—that's what they called her—helped her mother run the household, looking after her brothers and sisters, cleaning house, and cooking meals. The neighbors' twenty-year-old son cast his eyes upon the girl; the Gorettis had very close ties to his family. The young man, Alessandro Serenelli, first courted her, then tried to seduce her, and one day assaulted her. Marietta put up a fight, whereupon he stabbed her repeatedly in the belly with an awl. Marietta was taken to the hospital in the town of Nettuno, where surgery was performed without anesthesia. She died the following day, July 6, 1902. She was not yet twelve. She forgave her murderer before dying. Serenelli was convicted of the crime, served twenty-seven years in prison, repented, joined the Order of Friars Minor Capuchin as a lay brother, worked in various monasteries, and died in Macerata in 1970.

A teenage girl murdered in her home. A case of rape and violence against women. I was ashamed ever to have misconstrued her, to have come so perilously close to mocking the victim. So I decided to go.

I left Rome, to which I had traveled for work, aboard a little train that huffed and puffed up into the wintry Apennines, taking four hours to reach Falconara Marittima, north of Ancona. After dinner, we drove up to Corinaldo. At the Teatro Goldoni, which was packed with a rapt audience, we talked about Maria Goretti, Bishop Franco and I: two natives of Crema on an evening in the Marche thoughtfully discussing the story of a young woman who had grown up in that town— sadly an all-too-relevant story because certain horrors are still with us. A great deal has been written about Marietta— everyone in Corinaldo still calls her that, without "saint" and without surname. In 1985, Giordano Bruno Guerri published the book *Povera santa, povero assassino* (*Poor Saint, Poor Murderer*), setting forth the opinion that her idealization and canonization were due to the desire—first on the part of the Fascists and later on the part of the Catholic Church—to create a peasant icon of moral integrity that could be held up in opposition to the changes in lifestyle and morality. The book stirred up controversy and much discussion.

Corinaldo, an enchanting medieval village that unfolds uphill, is the site of the Lanterna Azzurra discotheque, where on the night of December 8, 2018, just before a rapper was scheduled to begin his concert, six people were killed and fifty-nine were injured when a balustrade collapsed; someone had let off a canister of pepper spray, unleashing a panicky stampede. We talked about that as well, about young people and an Italy that occasionally veered into the realm of the incomprehensible for us adults. We talked about teenagers and the predators who circle around them, today even more than in the past. We also talked about the Church with a capital *C*, which sometimes struggles to understand and keep up; and the church with a small *c*, which instead understands perfectly. Maria Goretti isn't an asexual banner of some otherworldly purity; she was just a generous and kindhearted girl who never got the chance to grow up.

After the meeting, I was asked if I wanted to pay a visit to Marietta's mortal remains, which were housed in the nearby church. I said, "It's late, it's eleven p.m., the church must be closed." The organizers replied, "Let's ring the doorbell, you never know." So we did. A young nun came to answer the door, smiling, without her headpiece; Apostolic Sisters of the Good Shepherd, she explained. She'd been there for the meeting in the theater, so she knew everything already. She turned on the lights. Marietta—her earthly remains, small as she had been—were lying there, and we stayed for a little while. The tomb of her murderer, Alessandro Serenelli, was at the far end of the room, on the left. Small churches, small saints. As we left, I asked the nun, as she turned out the lights, "I'm not a priest, I'm not a theologian, I'm not a historian. What am I doing here?" She looked at me, taken aback. "Don't worry about that. If Marietta called you, there must be some reason."

30. Because we're too indulgent with crooks, but we can spot them instantly

The propensity to commit fraud is not an Italian trait, though some hecklers may say otherwise. But there was a time—I'll leave it to you to say whether or not that period is over—when a certain brilliant dishonesty was considered, more or less explicitly, to be a form of intelligence and therefore to be admired.

We Italians are rather good at recognizing con artists and scoundrels. But frequently we observe them with a mixture of detachment and amusement, as if they were some sort of sideshow attraction. Indignation? Maybe some other time.

There are two explanations for this attitude, if you ask me. The first comes very close to resignation: we know that only in vanishingly rare instances will our indignation result in any sanction or punishment, and we don't want to get angry without the likelihood of achieving some result. The second explanation points more in the direction of a wily cunning: we know that someday we, too, will be judged. Our indulgence is a sort of preventive self-absolution.

Incompetence is another characteristic that rarely escapes our notice. A country full of gifted craftspeople—talented in the use of thoughts, words, sounds, images, foods, objects, and ideas—can hardly fail to recognize an overweening apprentice. Yet in recent years, there have been those who've tried to persuade us that knowledge and expertise are faults—just think of certain populists, conspiracy theorists, and Luddites—and many have fallen for it.

Our frightening brush with the coronavirus ought to have convinced us once and for all that experts are good for something. Attacked by an invisible enemy, we turned to physicians, nurses, scientists, and political decision makers (amid the embarrassed silence of shamans and antivaxxers, who waited for the pandemic to subside before resuming their ravings). Likewise, however, when it comes to deciding whether to institute a universal basic income, evaluating the impact of a new railroad line, or bailing out an airline—that's right, Alitalia—we would be well advised to place our trust in someone who understands the labor market, the railroads, or the airline industry. It takes more than honesty for people to do their jobs well. They must also be competent.

How often in recent years have ignorance and hasty improvisation been brandished as though they were campaign medals? They've been welcomed with rounds of applause and votes. How could such a thing happen? Could it possibly have been because the competent, in Italy, had lost the trust of the masses and aroused suspicion? This time, too, I have a twofold answer.

Some experts have confused competence (a virtue) with vanity (a venial sin). Think of the televised processions of virologists and epidemiologists: at first people applauded, intimidated, but then they started to get annoyed; whereas other people of great expertise—and this is a far more serious transgression—have in recent years displayed such qualities as arrogance, greed, and low cunning. It's happened in many professions, in manufacturing, in universities, and in mass media. Some very capable people have failed, however, to understand that just knowing isn't enough; you need to be able to *convey*, make ideas clear without trying to drive them into people's heads. This is how the human soul operates: if we like someone, we tend to forgive a great deal from them, but if we don't like them, we hold them to account for every slightest fault. If a good doctor treats us arrogantly, we forget how competent he may be. The same goes for magistrates, engineers, and journalists.

The second explanation for the temporary triumph of incompetence is bound up with politics. Ruthless characters of every political color have done their best to convince us that experience and knowledge are superfluous—indeed, outright harmful. The hallmark of the elite, the way the ruling class holds the people at bay: honesty, engagement, and enthusiasm should be more than good enough! It has become clear that that's just not true. Enthusiasm, engagement, and honesty are indispensable, but unless they're accompanied by competence, they bring only confusion and uncertainty. Even Senator Nicola Morra of the Five Star Movement has admitted it: "We should reflect carefully on how best to prevent illogical thinking and mere incompetence, irrationality, and ineptitude from triumphing at all levels." One is tempted to say: it was about time.

The trick of populism, in the 2010s, worked in part because it rested on an unmentionable suspicion shared by certain shallow foreigners: perhaps Italian governments—both national and local—are superfluous and in any case need not be taken seriously. Many Italians, more or less consciously, believe that hospitals, public transport, the armed forces, the schools, and the entire social safety net are in and of themselves all that we need. An actual government? Cabinet ministers? The regional governments? Mere placeholders. Not all that important.

That's nonsense. And in the horrifying months of the pandemic, we've had proof of that fact: no organization can

function without leadership. Yet many Italians believe otherwise and will continue to think so, until a trauma or some
other unpleasant experience teaches them to think twice. We
certainly hope it never happens again, obviously. It would be
too high a price to pay just to teach a collective lesson.

31. Because we have a public school system, the ultimate social blender

Italy's new *didattica a distanza* (distance learning) system is identified with the acronym DAD, which is English for "papa." We ought to have named it MUM (Mamme Ufficialmente Malmesse), or MOM (Mothers Officially Miserable). In fact, it has been the mothers of Italy who have tended to the ramshackle home education complex over the trying year of the pandemic—and who will continue to do so.

We've heard a great deal of talk about desks on wheels, plexiglass partitions, flexible school hours, and reduced class sizes. One thing we know for sure: Italy was the first to shut down and the last to open back up. For families with school-age children, more should have been done. It's not clear why children could be allowed to get together blithely in parks, at summer camps, and on beaches—but not at school.

We underestimated the impact of the lockdown on the youngest members of society. The attention of politicians, the mass media, and public opinion has been focused on two other generations: the generation of grandparents, so vulnerable in terms of health care, and the generation of parents, dealing with the collapse of the family income. Less thought has been devoted to the children. They seemed physically and psychologically robust; they were bound to do just fine. With hindsight, however, we can now say it: how wrong we were.

Children and teenagers have been deprived of the social side of school, the fun part, leaving them to deal only with the rest of it (studying, homework, and grades). The burden of this new

development has come to rest partly on the shoulders of teachers, who've been forced to reinvent themselves (many have succeeded, some have fallen short, and a few never bothered to
try). But the real weight came down on the mothers, who've
been forced to combine working from home, doing the work of
running the household, and helping their children with their
schoolwork.

Out of eight million Italian students, 850,000 lack the basic
tools for distance learning; of the rest, 57 percent are forced to
share those tools with other family members. And this teaching
method cuts out the most vulnerable in society: the disabled,
students at high risk of dropping out of school entirely, families with low literacy levels (for elementary and middle school
students, distance learning demands parental involvement).
And then there's the general sensation of loss and abandon-
ment. Paola A., an elementary school teacher, told me about a
little girl who refuses to do her homework unless a photograph
of her teacher is placed in front of her.

The public school system is the ultimate national social
blender, the place where people meet others, mix and mingle,
provide one another with support, get and give help. And that's
not limited to the elementary, middle, and high school years: it
often endures for the rest of their lives.

The more complex Italy at large becomes, the more important the Italian school system becomes. That is where young
people spend most of their time: with their classmates, friends,
teachers, and school staff. The opinion and advice of another
student or a good teacher, at a certain age, have a power and
influence that we can't even begin to imagine—that is, unless
we think back and remember that we, too, were once that age.

Public school in Italy is a bridge, a boundary, a truce, a counseling center, and a shelter, today, just as it always has been. Boasting of strict treatment in the classroom and heaping piles of homework on the students is tantamount to admitting defeat from the outset; it's a tacit admission that you don't know how to educate them. Many teachers are discouraged, because teaching is a challenge: if a classroom exerts centripetal force—a steady beam of gravity, summoning students together—smartphones are centrifuges, scattering them inexorably. And distance learning has only complicated matters further.

To help teachers make the effort, the institution as a whole needs to be encouraged, better financed, better organized, and streamlined (not even Covid has been able to conquer the intrinsic formalism of the Italian school system). These objectives, unfortunately, do not seem to be priorities for Italy's political class. Political parties and governments are constantly and frantically searching for points of immediate consensus and approval, and they try to buy that consensus through shortsighted measures. School is an investment, and if it's struggling, that's at least partly our fault. We spend so much time arguing about taxes and so little thinking clearly about education.

The schools are the last remaining sites of national formation. Either you create Italy there, or you give up trying. Yet Italy is in the very lowest ranking among the thirty-seven members nations of the Organization for Economic Co-operation and Development (OECD) in terms of government spending on education (we spend more money paying interest on the public debt). Many of our forty-one thousand school buildings are in miserable condition. We have one of the highest dropout rates (a million in ten years) and the lowest rate of university-level degree completion in Europe, lagging behind even Romania. Does that seem normal to you?

I am Spider-Man's uncle. I realized this years ago when my nephew Carlo—now the young father of Bruno and Pietro—came home from school with a note from the teacher stating (verbatim), *The student was caught in the act of climbing the wall with the intent of entering class through the window.* With admirable modesty, the young man—a tenth grader in scientific high school—had explained, "The window was quite low."

The memory of my acrobatic nephew led me to take a new look at a message I received from a reader, Cinzia C. A teacher, Cinzia sent me a selection of disciplinary notes from the Italian classroom ledgers. I have no idea from where she dug them up nor how far back they date, but they're fascinating.

> Student S.C. left class prior to the end of the period after taking a picture of the blackboard with his cell phone, promising to study the lesson at home that evening.

> Student A., absent from the classroom since 12:03 p.m., returned at 12:57 p.m. with a new haircut.

> Student A., during recess, performed an imitation of Benito Mussolini, complete with fez and black shirt, issuing a declaration of war against a rival school located across the street.

> Student L.P., during a phys ed class, chased his female classmates, waving a toilet brush in the air.

> Student S. entered the classroom after a twenty-minute absence to go to the bathroom by kicking

the door in, performing a somersault, and then aim-
ing an imaginary pistol at the teacher, announcing,
"You are hereby under arrest."

Student T. excused his absence the previous day by
writing *I thought it was Sunday.*

What can we say in the presence of these flashes of school
life in the twenty-first century? Maybe this: They're highly
reminiscent of the 1970s, for instance. And we've missed out
on them during the Covid pandemic, a time of deserted classrooms. School, of course, is not just this, but it's *also* this. It's
being together and building up a treasury of memories. Anyone who denies that is a hypocrite—or else never had children
of their own or nieces and nephews; or perhaps is a very boring
person. Or maybe they're all these things put together: a boring hypocrite without children, nieces, or nephews.

32. Because we have nursery schools, and we produced Maria Montessori

When the Fondo Ambiente Italiano (FAI), Italy's National Trust, held its National Days in 2020, my friend Annalisa Doneda (we went to high school together, and she's the head of the FAI delegation in Crema) did yeoman's work: she convinced landowners to open venerable old *palazzi* to the public, she recruited volunteers, she gathered hard-to-find information, and she organized guided tours. One stop on the itinerary was the municipal Montessori nursery school, where many long years ago I spent a happy childhood: I tidied up after making a mess, I made peace after quarreling, I set the table for meals and cleared away afterward, and I chased little girls through the garden, waving fat earthworms to scare them. And every time I entered or exited the nursery school, I looked up at the banana tree.

Banano, in Italian. Banana tree—though back then it didn't produce bananas. Nowadays—could it be because of climate change?—it *does* produce bananas: a bunch of tiny ones. The big banana tree still stands there, facing south, next to the front entrance, gracing the low orange facade. It wasn't the garish color of the facade that left me uneasy: not at the turn of the 1960s, when I was attending nursery school; not in the mid-1990s, when I was taking my son, Antonio, there; and not in these strange 2020s. What I've always found striking is the banana tree itself: its presence, its incongruous appearance, its immense, drooping leaves, bold and brash in summer, disheartened in winter. It seems as if this banana tree in the Po

Valley is asking all the people going by "Hey, what am I doing here?"

The answer to that question remained a mystery to me for half a century. Then Annalisa took on the job. After overcoming her initial misgivings—why was I worried about the banana tree, as opposed, say, to the art treasures of Crema?—she did her research; she determined that in all likelihood the banana tree was an African symbol, an emblem of colonial conquest, naively imperial in aspiration; hence, Fascist in spirit and origin. The construction of the nursery school, in fact, dates back to 1935. It was named in honor of Crown Prince Umberto of Italy. The royal coat of arms and the dedications to Il Duce are gone now. The banana tree, cautious and self-effacing, still stands. Politics, luckily enough, has no time to waste on trees.

I observe the banana tree with respect. It has seen generations of Crema's children come and go, and they all remember the tree. I have no idea of the average life span of a Po Valley banana tree, but I'll confess that I'm impressed by this tree's resilience. I imagine that at least once I must have asked, on my way into the nursery school, "Mamma, what's that?" And my mamma, Carla, would have replied, "A banana tree." If she had told me it was a baobab or a birch, it would have made no difference to me. As far as I was concerned, bananas grew at the fruit vendor's shop, so it was just a funny case of similar names. I didn't really think that the tree had anything to do with bananas.

I read Maria Montessori's life story, by no means a simple one. She was born more than 150 years ago, on August 31, 1870. She was a rebellious student, who went on to take a degree in medicine and study psychiatry. She had an unhappy love affair and a son she long ignored; she always dressed in black; she spent years in Spain, initially supported Mussolini, and attempted to bring together religious education with pedagogical principles. And then she had the formidable idea of placing the child at the center of the entire education plan. That meant giving free rein to the instincts of little ones, who should be observed and guided, not forced to learn. This is an Italian woman we can proudly display to the world, a fighter, a pain in the neck, a feminist ahead of her time, a visionary, a national treasure, a collective grandmother (with a grandmother's hairdo), a perfect portrait to be featured on Italian banknotes.

The first Casa dei Bambini—Children's House—was established in 1907, but the Crema nursery school did not take that name until 1953. As of this writing, there are sixty-five thousand Children's Houses around the world. In Italy, there are not nearly enough. The method developed by Maria Montessori is the most admired, adopted, and imitated pedagogical model for one very simple reason: it works.

The starting point is this: confidence needs to be expressed in each child. Children shouldn't be hovered over, obligated, bored, manhandled, or petted and fussed with. A child should be allowed spontaneity, made to feel free in a setting where everything—the spaces, the furnishings, the objects—is built to their size. The teacher must offer a brief initial explanation and then watch without interfering. "Never help a child with a task at which he feels he can succeed," Montessori warned us. "When you have solved the problem of controlling the attention of the child, you have solved the entire problem of its education," she added (ah, if only the ministers and secretaries of education were as wise as she).

꧁꧂

I started at Crema's Montessori nursery school in 1959, and I stayed there until 1962. I remember a miniworld of small tables, lightweight chairs, coatracks no taller than me. I remember fascinating activities (serving a table, what a privilege!). I remember the wooden jigsaw puzzles, especially the one with all the regions of Italy (I always tried to jam Umbria into the space where Basilicata was supposed to go). I remember my teacher, Anna Mancastroppa, who addressed each of us individually by name, almost never speaking to the assembled class. I remember her kind smile as she spoke to us in a serious voice, as if we were grown-ups. I remember that she would ask us to take responsibility for our actions, because she wanted us to understand the difference between right and wrong. Everything else I learned, over the course of the rest of my life, proved far less important.

The Montessori was the secular nursery school of Crema; it was taken over by the town government in 1975. The religious nursery school of the Handmaids of Charity was across the street. Our little Tiber, here in Crema, was called Via Bottesini. Every now and then I go back there, on the flimsiest of excuses. I went to tell fairy tales to my son, Antonio's, class, with permission from his teacher, Carolina. Some time ago I took the principal a copy of my book *Italiani si diventa* (*Italian Is Something You Become*). On the cover was my official year-end photograph, the one delivered to family: a white smock, neatly combed hair, and an angelic complexion, possibly retouched and in any case unsettling in its perfection.

In another photograph I'm holding hands with my sister, Paola, two years younger than I. Paola is smiling seriously;

I seem calm and protective. Actually, though, I'm told that I was a pretty active youngster. My filthy knees would certainly confirm that report. That photograph is evidence—tiny, personal, and remote—of a belief of Maria Montessori: "Children, if placed in a suitable environment and presented with the right material, quickly cease being noisy and excitable and are soon transformed into calm and tranquil creatures, happy to work." That was exactly what happened to so many of us. I don't know how the teachers at the Crema Montessori nursery school managed it, but they did.

These days, the children aren't as neatly brushed and combed, but they seem every bit as cheerful, and there is a hum of busy activity. The Crema Montessori nursery school was further renamed in 2003, after a former principal, Iside Franceschini, and it now has a student body of 149 children. It feels as if you're walking into a miniature city, where everyone has something to do. Obviously, the children are there to *play*. But also to wash dishes, do laundry, shine shoes; push a meal trolley and serve their fellow children ("food server" is a much-sought-after assignment).

I remember one recent visit. I noticed a little boy—about four years old—clutching a knife that, if set on end, might have stood at half his height.

"What's he doing?" I asked apprehensively.

"He's slicing bread," the principal, Emilia Caravaggio, replied.

"Well, isn't there some danger that he might cut himself?"

"Oh, yes, every so often the children do nick themselves, but it's never particularly serious. They learn that knives are dangerous, that knives should be handled with care."

Every time I leave the Montessori nursery school, I feel relieved and I think to myself: What if this were the real school that all Italians attend? Where they would learn to face challenges on their own, to invent and to build, to make themselves useful, to argue and then make peace, to know right from wrong? Pity the fools and ignore the troublemakers. Avoid kissing up to and being kissed up to by the authorities. Do their best not to hurt themselves.

33. Because we have the national health service and family doctors

The Vespa with a Cremona province license plate—number CR19493, three forward gears, headlight on the mudguard—is still circulating on the local roadways, but the driver is no longer with us. Dr. Maurizio Tonghini, a local general practitioner, born in 1928, made house calls every morning and in every season of the year on a yellow scooter with a black satchel under the seat, zipping this way and that through the city of Crema. He spent his afternoons receiving patients in his clinic. That was his life for forty years, from the mid-1950s until the mid-1990s. He had a map of East Africa on the wall behind him, glass-front shelves, a desk covered with ballpoint pens, an exam table, and a round adjustable-height stool. I still have that stool. Every so often I wonder how many tens of thousands of people sat on it, mouths open and tongues extended, blood test results in hand, their hearts racing anxiously, their backs aching.

Dr. Paolo Tonghini, born in Udine in 1896, was Maurizio Tonghini's father. After completing his high school studies at the Liceo Manin in Cremona, he enrolled in the medical school of Parma and was then shipped out to the front in the First World War. Upon his return he finished his interrupted medical education, took his degree, met Palmira, a young woman from Piadena three years his junior, and married her. He worked as a general practitioner and she as a schoolteacher. The young couple came to live in Madignano, just outside Crema. Palmira looked like the girls on soapboxes: oval face, green eyes, hair pulled back in a bun. Dr. Tonghini wore small, round spectacles and a lab coat that hung down to his feet, took correspondence courses to keep up with the progress of medical science, played the piano, was unbeatable at chess, detested hypochondriacal matrons, and never took payments from the poor.

Dr. Paolo Tonghini was my maternal grandfather; Dr. Maurizio Tonghini was my uncle and, for many years, my family doctor. Would it be possible these days to practice medicine in that manner? Certainly not. But family doctors are still an important resource. To spend a portion of the available EU funds to reinvent an indispensable profession would not be a bad idea.

The family doctor is a sentinel, a guard standing sentry on the public health, "the hub of all primary care," as they say nowadays, the professional of informed intuition and first diagnosis. Is the family doctor still a figure of relevance to modern society? Or has the profession been rendered obsolete by Google, specialists, and the emergency room? Paola Pedrini, the secretary of the Federazione Italiana Medici di Medicina Generale (Italian Federation of General Practitioners), did her best to sound reassuring: "The family doctor puts the whole puzzle together. The specialist, however skilled he may be, sees just his piece of the puzzle. We have the whole picture: the clinical, personal, family, social, and economic situation—and a doctor-patient relationship with a basis in empathy."

A relationship and an empathy that the Covid epidemic has damaged badly. Our family physicians have appeared solitary, helpless, and bewildered. And, with them, so have we.

My impression is that at the beginning of the pandemic, our family doctors were navigating by guesswork. Physicians were examining patients without donning personal protection.

Maria Teresa Arrigoni, who has a roster of 1,600 patients, practices medicine in Milan; she recalled buying a plastic face shield in the gardening section of her local Brico, a DIY chain. "After a while we were instructed, 'Stay in your clinics, monitor your patients by phone and by email.' So that's what we did. We made sure we were available by phone from eight in the morning till eight at night. But at that point, many of us were already infected. And some of us died."

Things didn't go all that much better with the swabs: at first tests were done only after a patient had been accepted into an ER; family physicians couldn't even prescribe them. Then, in Lombardy, the Agenzie di Tutela della Salute (ATS, or Health Protection Agencies), the public health structures, decided to step in. They asked general practitioners to identify patients who needed to have a swab done if they presented a concerning clinical picture or urgently needed to return to work. But as we know, there was a shortage of swabs, certainly inadequate in the face of the demand.

The family doctor didn't take to their heels in 2020 but held their ground. The sentinel had spotted the enemy but largely lacked the resources to raise the alarm. Even the governor of Lombardy, Attilio Fontana, admitted as much: "Are you asking me to admit we were wrong? Probably so; in recent years we've overlooked family doctors. We are going to introduce a major action plan to reinforce their ranks. They are the first firewall in terms of public health for our communities, and we will strengthen them." One is tempted to say: Better late than never. But Lombardy's regional government, alas, failed to behave accordingly.

Why is family medicine managed by the regional governments in Italy rather than being treated as a medical specialty on the national level like all the others? Why does the family doctor not expand his jurisdiction? Alessandro Inzoli, an oncologist in Lodi who contracted Covid, recovered, and went back to work, commented, "There is a hospital-centric view of things in Lombardy and elsewhere. Family doctors, unless they wish to become mere paper pushers drawing up medical referrals, must demand an expansion of their field of responsibility. As things stand currently, they're weighed down by the burden of administrative tasks, and far too many medicines can be prescribed only by hospital staff physicians. Many pharmacies are authorized to perform certain simple laboratory tests for payment. Only a very few family doctors are equipped to do the same thing. My father, Biagio, was a family doctor in Crema. In the early 1970s, in his clinic, he administered electrocardiograms, electroencephalograms, and chest X-rays. Many of his colleagues today have nothing more than a blood pressure cuff. Pulse oximeters, portable ultrasounds: Why don't we see more of them?"

Why is the role played by the general practitioner so fundamental? "Because in the case of new epidemics—which are likely, not just a possibility—patients need to be kept out of hospitals as long as practicable; they are places where infections occur and viruses can be transmitted. The emergency room isn't the proper front door to the health care system. That door has a name; it's called the family doctor," explained Renata Gili, a physician in Turin specializing in public health (she, too, contracted Covid on the job and has since recovered). She now works in Bologna, at the Fondazione GIMBE (Gruppo Italiano per la Medicina Basata sulle Evidenze, or Italian Group for Evidence-Based Medicine). The foundation president, Nino Cartabellotta, said, "Change must start from within the category. The general practitioner is currently a freelance professional who has an official working relationship with the national health service; it's a peculiar status. In order to revise that status, there need to be major, overarching contractual and organizational changes. Family medicine must change its stripes, but does it have the will to do so?"

"No one can be saved alone," said Pope Francis on a rain-drenched St. Peter's Square on Easter 2020. If we have been saved, it's at least in part thanks to our physicians, in hospitals and out. We owe them a debt of gratitude. One way of honoring that debt? Let's help them to help us.

34. Because our policemen don't glare at us, though sometimes they should

In the old days, a car zigzagging down the street was a clear indicator: either the driver was a beginner, or he was drunk. These days, it's a distinguished gentleman sending a text. A study done a few years ago found that one young Italian out of four had taken a selfie while driving and one out of three had posted on and checked social media while at the wheel of a car. Today that number has probably risen to three out of four. Mothers, fathers, and grandparents are no better. What's more, they check Google Maps because they don't know their way around and are afraid of getting lost.

The scenario is no different in any Italian city. Compact cars zip this way and that like so many hysterical mosquitoes while their drivers gab away amiably, cell phone pressed to their ear or managing their online lives. Some fail to go when the stoplight turns green; others fail to stop when it turns red. Many see pedestrians only at the last minute, if they see them at all. Motorcyclists are no better. We've all seen them, high-wire daredevils holding one handlebar with their left hand while typing out texts with their right (if they're left-handed, the other way around). What will happen now that the streets are filled with electric scooters?

Why aren't these behaviors punished? Out of an excess of tolerance, I'm afraid. But tolerance is like cholesterol: a little bit is fine, too much is harmful.

Prior to the coronavirus outbreak, twenty million euros were missing from the coffers of the city of Milan. That money was the revenue due from traffic tickets, fines levied but not paid. Today, I imagine, that cash is more necessary than ever. Do you want to find money? Just ticket everyone you catch driving while using their smartphone. And not just in Milan: everywhere.

Here's a question: If *we* can all see them, why do city police seem to have a blind spot? Do you want to know how many accidents are caused by this bad habit? The city of Shenzhen, China, to which I traveled in October 2019, has a population of twenty-two million, seven times the metropolitan area of Milan. An acquaintance of mine told me that he jaywalked in Shenzen while the pedestrian crossing signal was red; by the time he reached the opposite side of the street, a fine had already been imposed and collected via a debit to his bank account (by means of facial recognition and payment by WeChat). None of us is calling for the introduction of anything like that. But we can and we should do more than we are doing now.

This scourge—this form of collective idiocy?—has been the subject of hundreds of articles, lectures, conferences, investigations, conversations, and even provocations; nothing can be done, it seems. The likelihood of being fined for improper smartphone use while driving is vanishingly small, at least in Italy. Yet Article 173 of the Traffic Code could not be any clearer. Why doesn't anyone do anything? Why don't the municipal police—the traffic wardens in Milan are known as the *ghisa*, the "cast iron"—put a halt to it? At the very least, why don't they give it a stern glare? The reason is that in order to give a stern glare, they'd need to see it happening. And in order to see it happening, they'd have to get out onto the streets more frequently.

I usually go home from my office at *Corriere della Sera* on the Metro, but that day I was driving. I was going from Via Solferino to my home in Milan's Solari district, and on my way I counted how many bicycles had their taillight turned on: four out of twenty-nine, or 13.8 percent. All the rest were nothing but shadows in the darkness. For the most part, the cyclists were delivery riders on their rounds, but they were also workers returning home, young people, mothers with children— none with a safety light on the back. It was winter: the days were short, the evening began early. The bicycles appeared without warning in my field of view, the rider almost invariably wearing a dark jacket and with no running lights.

It happens every day, in every season. Everyone knows it, and no one does anything about it.

In Italy, there are rules that are blithely ignored. That was the case with drunk driving until the sheer number of fatalities forced us to take stern measures. This is still the case with the obligatory use of rear seat belts in cars. A taxi driver in Rome heard the click of my seat belt, whereupon he turned around and looked at me with chagrin: "You don't trust me. . . ."

Oh, I trust you, I explained, but if you slam on the brakes while I'm looking at my phone—as all passengers in all cabs do, by definition—then I'm going to bang my nose against the back of your headrest. But if I fasten my seat belt, then we'll all rest a little easier.

He replied, "You know, you have a point!"

The case of bicycle lights is every bit as mysterious. Bicyclists are especially vulnerable in city traffic: they ought to have every interest in making themselves as visible as possible, as is the practice in the cities of northern Europe. But here, zero—as if Italian darkness isn't as dark, the cars are not as threatening, the asphalt is softer and more accommodating. The idea of a traffic warden, a police officer, or a carabiniere stopping a cyclist without lights? Science fiction.

The most stunning cases are the cyclists delivering food. I encountered a pair on Via California, two young African men with backpacks bearing the insignia of the Glovo food-delivery app. The first man hadn't turned on his lights; the second didn't even have any. I asked whether their employer required them to have lights on their bikes, seeing as they were delivering at night; I received only evasive answers. A few days later, I read an interview in which Glovo announced that its delivery riders would now be covered by Istituto Nazionale per l'Assicurazione contro gli Infortuni sul Lavoro (INAIL, Italy's worker's compensation agency). Well, the thought does occur: If we were to prevent workplace accidents rather than compensate workers for them, so much the better. Right?

35. Because we know how to think with our hands and work with our thoughts

I understand why retired men love watching construction sites. It's nice to see work being done well.

In Italy, many people do their work well, with precision and passion. When you read the statement of a contractor or an entrepreneur declaring that Italian craftsmen and factory workers are incomparable in terms of skill, don't think they're just trying to get in good with the labor force. They are almost always expressing sincere gratitude and, in a sense, declaring their reliance and trust.

Good Italian workers think before taking action. If they disagree, they say so. If they find themselves in a work environment where their input is considered insubordination, that doesn't make them happy and they say so. I realized this while visiting car factories in Puglia, cosmetics plants in Lombardy, wineries in Piedmont, carpentry shops in Trentino and Alto Adige, shipyards in Liguria, crafts workshops in Tuscany, textile mills in Campania, and mechanical plants and construction sites all over the country.

If you want evidence of the sheer intelligence of the manual worker, talk to any foreigner who has come to live in Italy. With a few exceptions, interactions with artisans, tradespeople, and builders are described with an admiration that borders on shameless flattery. I have friends in London who still remember when the mechanic Franco laid his hands upon their old car or when the seamstress Gabriella altered a dress or suit. In American, British, and northern European books about Italy, there is unfailingly a chapter about the artisans the author has watched working either in their own homes or elsewhere. One Finnish author, Ella Kanninen, in *Minun Italiani* (*My Italy*) even included photographs.

There was a period in the 1960s and 1970s when Italian authors focused deeply on the moral and aesthetic dimensions of manual labor: Primo Levi, Paolo Volponi, Ottiero Ottieri, Giovanni Giudici. It's not hard to sense the underlying political motivation, but what comes through, more than anything else, is admiration. Admiration for work done well.

I have always been struck by the Italian pride—in many cases, joy—in performing one's profession precisely and well; thinking up an artwork or an object one day and fabricating, manufacturing, or simply shaping it the next day. In my family, as I'll describe later, we had a passion for building: renovating more than constructing from the ground up. I've always noticed the great respect my father—himself a respected professional, a notary, and therefore, in Italy, comparable to a lawyer—always showed to masons and bricklayers, whatever their age: he understood that they knew how to do things that he couldn't; that the walls they built, every bit as much as the deeds he drafted, were made to endure.

One legend of my childhood was the master builder Santo Piloni. When I was a child, I thought his first name and surname—Santo, meaning "holy" or "saint," and Piloni, a modern pillar or ancient gateway—indicated the beatification in this life of his building skills. I later learned that Santo Piloni was simply his name. He had built our house, and he returned frequently to do various projects. When Santo Piloni spoke—standing on the front porch in his blue workman's overalls and his shirt spattered with mortar and plaster—we all stood in silence, listening raptly. Among all he said is one phrase I still recall, addressed to a young apprentice. It rhymed in dialect: *"Col cervèl, mìa col martèl."* Use your brain, not your hammer! Which is to say: first think it through, then pick up your tools.

I suggest we have those words carved over the main entrance of every Italian ministry for all to see.

36. Because our countryside never looks bored

There's a picture of me from 1960 in which I'm sitting at the wheel of a tractor. Nearly all the children in Lombardy have a picture of themselves sitting at the wheel of a tractor. Tractors are the mechanical pachyderms of the Western world. I imagine that in India's Rajasthan, children are photographed sitting on elephants. In the Po Valley, they sit on tractors.

That tractor—manufactured by a German company, Hanomag; the name was written in a vertical line down the front of the radiator—was simply gigantic. Or maybe I was just very small. The tractor was a fixture of the farm owned by my uncle Lazzaro, whom we all called Rino, in Offanengo, just off the main road. In that photograph my expression is a mixture of ecstatic and worried: that high off the ground, when you're three and a half years old, your emotions tend to be mixed. My grandmother Giovanna, my mamma, four aunts, and two uncles, all standing around the tractor, gaze at me proudly. I was the firstborn son of the youngest of seven siblings, the only grandson who bore the Severgnini surname. If I'd asked them to let me start the tractor and drive it to my nursery school, they'd have opened the front gate and cheerily waved me on my way.

Nearly every Sunday, for years and years, I went to the farmhouse. When I wasn't sitting on the tractor or romping in the hayloft, on the terrace, in the chicken house, or in the orchard, I'd be wandering around the barnyard. It was overrun, depending on the season, by various heaps of corn, wheat, hay, or sugar beets. The crops emitted intense odors, as did the stables, as did the kitchen, as did the stairs leading up into the terrace. In the fall, the smell of manure in the *rüdéra*, a fertilizer heap, penetrated powerfully everywhere. To me it remains a familiar scent, one I don't especially dislike; my city friends find it repugnant. Too bad for them; they're missing out.

My wife makes fun of me. All the paintings that I like—she claims—are green: fields outside Crema, Lombard mountains, lakes in the Bergamo region, Milanese parks, English gardens, American prairies. Even the Russian countryside, which is always depicted in the same manner: a melancholy expanse of green crisscrossed by narrow, mud-brown lanes. I possess a small painting that belongs to that genre, purchased in a Moscow market in 1991, and Ortensia can't stand it. I've been forced to move it preventively from one house to another in order to spare it the humiliation of the attic or even worse. Now it's in our Milan apartment, hanging in the guest bedroom. Our visitors are all required to notice it and sing its praises.

Green is the color that the human eye can most easily split into the greatest variety of shades. This is a natural consequence of the evolution of the species: our ancestors, for the sake of survival, were forced to learn to spot predators in among the greenery. Our attraction to this color, however, has other explanations. The most common one: green is restful and optimistic; it's evocative of ever-rejuvenating nature. In my case, there's a biographical variant. The countryside around Crema and the valleys above Bergamo, where I spent my childhood and adolescence, are monochromatic: green as far as the eye can see. Fields, mountains, riverbanks, trees, bushes, hedges, and crops range over every shade of the color, including olive green—though I'd be inclined to rule out the idea that olive trees grow in the Val Seriana and in the Lombard fields around Crema.

In my attraction to greenery, there's also a family component. The Severgnini have been tilling the soil for at least five hundred years: in the parish registers of Offanengo we found the birth certificate of "Gi. Jacomo Severgnini" (1520), the son of farmers. Every generation—and fifteen generations have passed—one of us has been authorized to pursue a different occupation. We have fielded crown prosecutors, court clerks, apothecaries, perfumers, teachers, businesspeople, restaurateurs, merchants, archpriests, even journalists. But the land attracts us; it's no accident that, immediately prior, I wrote that we, as a family, have "fielded" members of various professions. My son, Antonio, is also a farmer, my nephew Carlo has a degree in agricultural studies, and my nephew Francesco works in the sector of agricultural administration. I know the size of a *pertica*, used in land surveying, and I can tell a beech tree from a linden.

It's a unique life story, as is every life story. But I'm hardly an outlier: agriculture is the main substance of many Italian family histories. You can spot such families by how they look at the land: with fondness and respect but devoid of sentimentalism. The fields work, the fields understand, the fields sleep, and the fields awaken. Uncle Rino spoke of the fields and countryside as if of some demanding lover who often tested his temper. As a child, with my sister, Paola, and my brother, Francesco, I would jump in the hay and romp amid the corncobs left out to dry, often doing so without his genial approval. Only as he grew older did my uncle grow gentler: he'd stroll through his fields without worrying about whether to sell them or buy more. And he'd feed the ducks instead of shooting them.

The Italians who understand the fields are greater in number than the Italians who work them. Arable land in Italy is precious, and we're all keenly aware of it. Maybe a few greedy developers understand it, too, when they plan to put a useless apartment building on an otherwise lovely piece of land. It also became clear during the worst months of the pandemic. The land eyed the virus with derision; it won the battle without even fighting. But the land still had to be cared for, tended, worked, and prepared. Do you know who actually wrote the diaries of a country lockdown? Not farmers; they had too much work to do. The rural diaries were all written by artists and intellectuals who sought shelter and consolation in the midst of green nature. They were bucolic dilettantes; the professionals didn't have that kind of spare time.

The Italian fields are serious business. They are almost invariably the prizes of a hard struggle. We tore them out of hillsides and mountainsides, protected them from rivers and torrents, reclaimed them from swamps. The fertile countryside of Crema is the product of reclamation projects dating back to the eleventh century, the work of Benedictine and Cistercian monks who drained the marshes and bogs of Lake Gerundo, creating the network of irrigation ditches and canals crisscrossed by bridges and locks that we can still admire today.

In Italy, we farm thirty million acres of land, less than Germany (thirty-seven million acres) and France (seventy million acres). My wanderings through the fields have taught me that Italian farming contracts are renewed in November and that individual cows won't be offended if we group them together and just call them cattle. I've gotten to know individual farmers, and I've learned to admire the sheer determination and opinionated passion they bring to their profession. Often they can be dogmatic; but people who never take summer vacations and who are often up and about before sunrise have earned the right to be direct if not abrupt.

Italian agriculture is changing, as is our zootechnics. Our organic farming sector encompasses 4.5 million acres and seventy-two thousand farmers and farmworkers. Italy's agricultural food products bear such designations as DOP (Denominazione di Origine Protetta, or Protected Designation of Origin), IGP (Indicazione Geografica Protetta, or Protected Geographical Indication), and STG (Specialità Tradizionale Garantita, or Traditional Specialty Guaranteed), for a total of 304 designated foodstuffs ranging from *abbacchio romano* (Roman spring lamb) to the *zampone di Modena* (Modenese stuffed pig's trotter) along with 524 wines—a total of 828 designations, accounting for one-quarter of all those registered around the world. There are roughly twenty-five thousand agritourism farmstays, from Alto Adige to Sicily. In Lombardy, there are forty-four thousand individual farms. Ten thousand are run by women; about seven hundred by someone born abroad. Uncle Rino would be astonished. If he came back to visit, I'd step off the tractor of my memories, and I'd tell him: Situations change, and that's just fine. As long as the fields aren't bored, we're safe and sound.

37. Because work's demanding, but we can't do without it

Money plays a starring role in literature, television, movies, and music. "That's nothing new," you might say. From Plautus to Alberto Moravia, from Pink Floyd to Martin Amis (in both cases, the title is *Money*), from Madonna to Marilyn Monroe, and from Sergio Leone to *The Wolf of Wall Street*, a great many writers and artists have narrated, acted out, and sung the exploits of money. Perhaps in Italy, these days, we're less artistic, but we're certainly passionately interested in the subject.

Having money is a good thing, because it allows us *not* to have to think about money. If money becomes a source of worry—because there's too little, because there's too much—it stops becoming an opportunity and transforms, frequently, into an obsession. It can inspire a novel, but it's more likely to produce a neurosis.

These days our focus on money tends to be inversely proportional to our ability to access it. This is not merely an economic consequence of the pandemic; it's a more general condition of an entire generation, the one born in the last twenty years of the twentieth century. Anyone roughly thirty years old works very hard and earns, proportionately, relatively little. And money winds up occupying a disproportionately large space in their mind.

The impoverishment of Italian millennials took place with the consent—the euphoric consent, at least at first—of the interested party themselves. According to a bizarre form of work

ethic fostered in startups and on social media, it's impossible
to toil hard enough. Seventy- and eighty-hour workweeks are
(or were?) greeted with boundless enthusiasm; hence the constant commitment, the group spirit, the devotion to the mission statement, and, ultimately, the overriding need to be on
call every minute of the day and night. To some bosses, turning off your cell phone is an act of open insubordination.

Many young Italians have been urged to follow the example
of Elon Musk, who tweeted, "Nobody ever changed the world
on 40 hours a week." The correct number of hours, explained
the billionaire entrepreneur, "varies per person, but about 80
sustained, peaking above 100 at times." What can we say?
Musk has become incredibly wealthy and sends human beings
into space; those who imitate him become incredibly stressed
and send curses into the surrounding atmosphere when they
look at their pay stubs—if they receive any.

Seeking satisfaction from one's job is a legitimate expec-
tation, but the monetary compensation has to be adequate.
Too often, that's not the case. "Bosses and investors—not
workers—are the ones capturing most of the gains," wrote
Erin Griffith, a young reporter for the *New York Times*'s San
Francisco bureau. "I saw the greatest minds of my generation
log 18-hour days—and then boast about #hustle on Instagram.
When did performative workaholism become a lifestyle?"

Working from home, as we've seen, threatens to become just
one more pretext for further lowering salaries. Facebook has
wasted no time. Mark Zuckerberg devoted one of his virtual
public meetings to the subject of remote work in the Covid era
and made it clear that it is not likely to be a temporary phenomenon. There will be new hires, he announced, but salaries
will be calculated according to the employee's place of residence. Anyone who moves away from the Bay Area can expect

to earn less. For Facebook employees, this may not be a problem. But the decision will set a precedent. The ripples from a stone tossed into the water of Menlo Park will arrive in Italy eventually.

To say that young Italians are underpaid isn't an old-school socialist message; rather it is a postcapitalist observation. The new market appears dangerously out of balance, with a well-to-do elite who are able to motivate workers at the top and a broad, highly motivated base that is hardworking and underpaid. This applies to nearly all job sectors and professions: communications agencies, consulting studios, professional offices, and corporations. And medicine. We've given our wholehearted appreciation to our health care professionals over the many months of the Covid emergency, but their counterparts in Germany earn twice as much. And it's no accident that over the past eight years, nine thousand physicians have left Italy. Our health care system is short-staffed by ten thousand due to turnover and early retirements.

Some of you may be wondering: What can we do about it if the money's not there? If taxes on workers—basic taxes and social costs—are already punitive? We could answer that it hasn't always been this way and that sometimes it's as simple as the money going to the wrong people, people in vague positions who hunker down, jealously defending their acquired rights. Entitlements explain many of the delays in Italian development.

So what are the consequences? I alluded to the first at the outset: money is becoming a universal collective obsession, and that's not healthy. As far back as anyone can remember, and everywhere around the world, elections have been won or lost on either the merits or the perceived failure of the economy. And poverty, throughout history, has been the fuel of revolutions.

Revolution can happen again. The West, which had attained prosperity, is now an anxious place. Losing something is worse than never having had it at all.

The second consequence is bound up with the first. The new theoretical middle class—the educated neo-proletariat—threatens to fall under the sway of populists and demagogues. It's already happening elsewhere in Europe and in the United States. Do we want that for Italy, too? Then we need only stay on our present course.

Lots of money goes to those who complain. Very little at all goes to those who actually deserve it.

38. Because in every lab on Earth, there's a computer, a green plant, and an Italian

When, in Beijing in late 2019, I was awarded an honorary membership card and a light-blue sweatshirt bearing the logo AGIC—ASSOCIAZIONE GIOVANI ITALIANI IN CINA (Association of Young Italians in China), tears almost came to my eyes. There was a time when I was a sort of older brother with a friendly interest in their high-spirited adventures; today I am an aging father, worried about their future.

Half a million Italians have left Italy in the past ten years; half were young people under age thirty-four. It's a migration that has cost the nation sixteen billion euros, shaving nearly a percentage point off the gross domestic product—stunning numbers, if we still had it in us to be stunned by anything. The numbers slide past amid the screams of politicians and the surprises of the daily news cycle: our compatriots on distant shores have become little more than blurry figures, too far away to see clearly.

I got to know them well, I wrote a great deal about them, I met a great many of them: at least ten thousand between 1999 and 2010, during my trip around the world in conjunction with the blog/forum "Italians" for *Corriere della Sera*; 104 separate occasions, every time a pizza dinner and an evening spent together, from Shanghai, Buenos Aires, and Chicago to Melbourne, Moscow, and Lisbon, to get to know each other better. I've met so many other Italians since then, on different continents—at least three hundred during that Chinese visit, just before the Covid outbreak. The reason for my trip—as we've already mentioned—was a series of lectures on the Italian language. But in every city we made sure to get together (that was still possible back then): the Italians of the new great migration and a writer, somewhat less new, who has always considered them to be important.

Why do they leave, so many Italians, some young, others less so? There are latter-day Marco Polos who are eager to explore, fortunately. But there are also plenty of latter-day counts of Monte Cristo, escaping, turning their backs on unfair practices of all sorts (underpayment, obsolete corporate mechanisms, professions rooted in the past, lack of transparency in public administrations and universities). To say nothing of the state of women in the workplace: the employment crisis triggered by the Covid pandemic has shown us, once again, that young women have too little decision-making power and work too many hours (professional work, domestic work, and educating children). The ninth Annual Report on the Economics of Immigration by the Leone Moressa Foundation stated, "Italy is the country in the eurozone with the lowest employment rate in the age range 25–29. Only 54 percent of them have a job, in comparison with the European average of 75 percent."

Every major national issue winds up becoming background noise if it's left unsolved. The same is happening with our new great migration. Make no mistake: it's not wrong—in fact, it's perfectly right—for those who wish to explore the world professionally to do so, as long as it's a free choice and not made under duress. What's wrong is for this new way of life to go largely overlooked in the national narrative. Those who leave Italy realize that. As was once the case with Italians who'd emigrated to South America—as described in the song "Italiani d'Argentina" by Ivano Fossati—once again, today, Italians around the world ask from afar, "Hey, here we are. . . . Can you hear us from there?"

From Italy, there are relatively few responses.

A few universities respond, the ones that realize they need to reach out to the world. (Bocconi University and Milan's and Turin's Politecnico, or Polytechnic University, are active and well known in China.) There are responses from a fair number of corporations that see opportunities for development in the export sector and in international business in general. (I visited STMicroelectronics in Shenzhen and met with representatives of Fincantieri in Beijing, Luxottica in Guangzhou, Max Mara and Juventus in Hong Kong, and a variety of small and midsized companies everywhere.)

The president of the Italian Republic responds; Sergio Mattarella always has a fond thought for Italians abroad. Truth be told, the Foreign Ministry responds: a new generation of diplomats has come to understand that Italy's real strength is the Italians. It was their legs that carried out into the world the ideas that have conquered hearts and minds, eyes and stomachs (Italian cuisine, fashion, music, architecture, and technology); with our faces, smiling in spite of it all, we've presented those ideas at every latitude.

So who is it who's failing to respond? It's Italy. It's all of us, we who have so little to say about this far-flung community. And when we do respond, we give the impression that we're talking about some distant elite, whereas the Italians abroad come from every part of Italy, practice every profession, and come from every walk of life, social and economic. If we're unwilling to care about them out of respect or affection, let's do it out of self-interest; let's not forget that they constitute an enormous resource, something not all nations can count on. The bitterness and doubts that our emigrants abroad feel about Italy are, when all is said and done, tokens of love. No one would harbor a smoldering fury about a country they no longer cared about.

The furious arguments of recent years—from the political sunset of Silvio Berlusconi to the rise of Mario Draghi's national unity government by way of former prime minister Matteo Renzi's brief shooting star–like time in office, Matteo Salvini's League Party, the Five Star Movement's roller-coaster ride, and the embattled Giuseppe Conte governments—have convinced us that all that matters anymore is politics, but it isn't true. The trauma of the pandemic and the weaknesses of public institutions that it highlighted (administrative, economic, and health care shortcomings) prove that other issues matter as well. What matters first and foremost is the future of two new generations, about which we don't seem especially concerned as a collective; every proposal and every item of public spending seems instead to focus on achieving an immediate consensus. This lack of interest can be detected from our compatriots living in China, the United States, Russia, and Germany.

The Italians are still Italians, and they are shrewd.

39. Because we have old houses that need maintenance and tender loving care

My father, Angelo, familiarly known as Gino, was a notary by profession. At the end of his career he was proud of the three thousand wills he'd drawn up and deposited and the forty-four thousand deeds he had registered. But what he really enjoyed was houses: seeing them, touring them, fixing them up, renovating them, distributing them to his children and grandchildren. Once he'd run through all the houses he owned, he expanded his real estate activism to friends and acquaintances.

The notary Severgnini insisted that although financial investments are sometimes necessary, they aren't a source of satisfaction: you can't look out from the balcony of a bond or debenture. He didn't buy houses with a view to sell them, though he certainly sold a few; he bought them so he could let his imagination run wild. He knew the poetry of the terracotta roof tile and the melody of the rain gutter; he would stand raptly, enchanted by the sight of a painter at work on a ladder; he worried if he saw ivy spreading aggressively, because his sympathies always lay with the ancient wall, marked by the passage of centuries. The hours he spent on a construction site were his happiest hours; bricklayers, electricians, and carpenters understood him. His visits weren't considered an intrusion but a tribute of respect and admiration. My father would gather bent nails up from the ground, take them home, and straighten them. It wasn't the act of a cheapskate, it was a form of sincere respect.

Papà eventually became something of an expert: his knowledge of real estate joined the companion body of knowledge he possessed about farming, which was his by family right, and his juridical knowledge, the product of years of study and decades of practicing a profession. His passion for bricks—cored bricks, laterite bricks, concrete bricks, solid bricks, semisolid bricks, handmade bricks—extended to cobblestones and pavers: he could stand there for half an hour watching men laying a cobblestone street surface, something I do myself. That attraction led him to break one of the rules he'd learned from his farmer father, my grandfather Giuseppe: *"Bagai e teré i è mai asé. La cà dóma quela 'ndu sà stà."* Children and land are never enough; the house, only the one you live in.

I watched him build small houses in Sardinia in the 1970s, which he then distributed among us children, in the little settlement of Rena Majore in the township of Aglientu, not far from Santa Teresa Gallura. The young Gallurese builders—Peru and Muntoni, I still remember their surnames—were obliged to listen patiently to my father's philosophy of construction under the baking sun. But the houses were built well, and they're still standing.

I watched him build a house in the mountains in the early 1980s: the Lantana section of Dorga, on land purchased twenty years previously, looking out over the upper Val Seriana. It was a long, low house, without frills or plaster, like the classic *cascina* farmhouse. I remember when we were children that Papà would take us "to enjoy a picnic on our property": pride of ownership, planning, and panorama, wrapped up in one. Mamma Carla smiled as she made panini and hard-boiled eggs to take along.

I never saw him do it, but I knew he was fixing up the top-floor apartment in Crema from 1987 to 1988 while Ortensia and I, newlyweds, were living in London; then he moved on to the houses of my brother, Francesco, and my sister, Paola. He was impassioned and tireless. I would make fun of him, saying, "You're the only person I know who doesn't read a novel before going to sleep but a builder's estimate." He went so far as to fix up a number of row houses and sell them at cost to families with children, he'd gotten it into his head to repopulate a small outlying section of Crema (and, unbelievable but true, he did it). Then he pestered a series of mayors until one finally agreed to build a bike path to the development (and in the end, he got it done, paying with his own money for the drafting of the master plan). I watched him suffer when, in 1996, after Ortensia's and my return from the United States, we renovated the country house and failed to consult him frequently and thoroughly enough for his tastes. But he loved what we did with the place, and for twenty years he boasted that he'd made all the necessary decisions.

Dump trucks and scaffoldings were his tranquilizers, surveyors and architects his confidants. The best of them all was named Fiorenzo. With his help, Papà worked on farmhouses, signalmen's houses, farm outbuildings, apartments, warehouses, garages, rural buildings, stables, trattorias, city houses, country houses, cellars, and attic apartments. I saw him renovate wisely, restore shyly, and demolish decisively when there was no alternative. I remember that around 2000, he got it into his head to buy a tumbledown building on the Paullese state road near the bridge on the Adda River, with plans to renovate it. I dissuaded him. Every time we passed that building, he gazed at it with regret: Who knows how many bricklayers and masons, how many scaffoldings, how many conversations, how much there was to learn?

40. Because empty cities produce interesting sounds

From the windows of my office, I can see Crema's Piazza del Duomo: the cathedral is on the right of the square, the portico is on the left, the Torrazzo, the cathedral's bell tower, dead ahead, with its solemn and only approximately, and occasionally, accurate clock. Looking down at all hours, I see the city going past, on foot and on bicycle: grandparents with grandchildren, people carrying groceries in tote bags, farmers in town from their fields, groups of friends, college students, swarms of young boys and girls chattering intensely. A small knot of retirees gathers every morning at the corner of Via Vescovato to catch the first rays of sunshine peeking over the rooftops.

In the exceedingly strange spring of 2020, all that disappeared. The young people vanished, and so did the grocery bags; the farmers disappeared; the cafés and shops all shut down. The retirees were absent, though for two months the sun still shone unbroken on the cathedral's brickwork. Every so often, a solitary cyclist would emerge from the Torrazzo arch, face masked. From above I couldn't tell if the cyclist was a man or a woman, young or old. Only the pressure of the feet on the pedals and the direction of the gaze offered any clues. Young men stared straight ahead; everyone else looked down at the porphyry slabs sliding past beneath their tires.

When one pedestrian crossed paths with another, they'd steer clear of each other in a broad semicircular wheeling movement, very un-Italian. We normally tend to head straight for others, calling a greeting, shaking hands, in some cases hugging and kissing cheeks, unfurling smiles that may or may not be heartfelt. We live in a visual, auditory, tactile, olfactory society. We tend to trust our five senses more than we do grand overarching ideas (those we leave to the Germans). We use lots of pointless abstract words, that is certainly true. But to us, life is the light on objects and faces, the tangled scent of places, the sound of footsteps. We trust our eyes, our mouths, our noses, our ears, our hands, and our feet: to a fault sometimes. The days of Covid forced us to repudiate our senses.

At the beginning of the lockdown, when it was still permitted, I'd go out to the countryside after lunch for a walk with my wife, Ortensia. Our black Lab, Mirta, a great observer, would go with us. There were only a few infrequent clouds, a faint early-spring sunshine, flat fields and broad ditches, and the snow-covered mountains of Bergamo in the distance. Mirta, blithely unaware of the epidemic, chased nutrias, delighted to take in the smells of the budding spring. As we walked along the dirt roads, we'd cross paths with other strollers. They'd nod their heads. No one stopped to speak.

Later, in the afternoon, I'd go back to my office to write. In the evening, I'd go home. Occasionally, instead of crossing the square, I'd take a longer route. Walking in empty cities produces interesting sounds. Narrow lanes become sound boxes. You can hear footsteps, bicycles rattling and creaking on cobblestones, the hiss of tires on marble, shutters being fastened, voices and music from apartments. At the right hour, church bells rang, bravely, with a cheerfulness that seemed out of place.

One day I pushed on the cathedral's side portal. The door was open, and I walked in. The interior was dimly lit, but it's a space I know by heart: it's the church of my town's baptisms and funerals, our children's first Communions and our Sunday masses. In the apse of the left aisle there's a wooden crucifix dating back to the thirteenth century, to which the people of Crema feel a deep devotion; a bishop tried to relocate it once, a few years back, and he triggered a local insurrection. According to legend, in the harsh, chilly winter of 1448, the Ghibellines besieged in the cathedral tried to set fire to it in the hope of creating some warmth. Christ on the crucifix supposedly pulled up his legs, assuming his present-day position. Our ancestors prayed to the crucifix during the plague of 1630, so well described in Alessandro Manzoni's *The Betrothed*, and again during the epidemic of 1747. That evening in 2020, in the presence of Our Protector there was only one woman, sitting in the first pew. She moved slightly as she heard me come in, but she did not turn her head.

I walked back outside. As soon as I was in the open air, I heard, without warning, a deafening crash of music. I immediately knew where it was coming from. It was our town eccentric, who likes to pedal back and forth among Via XX Settembre, Piazza del Duomo, Via Mazzini, and Piazza Garibaldi. He'd mounted a large black speaker on his bicycle. In 2019, someone stole it; the people of Crema took up a collection to buy him a new, more powerful speaker. The musical cyclist mounted it on his cargo rack and took off: back and forth at all hours, at full volume. He loves old hits. That night, he was playing Umberto Tozzi's "Ti amo."

So life was going on. Excellent.

41. Because we want home delivery and we love having shops downstairs

Some time ago I was asked for a prediction about the future of shops in Italy. Journalists are used to being asked about topics of which they know nothing. I therefore kept my composure and calmly replied, "There will be fewer of them." It gives me no pleasure, that I will confess; but when asked, you answer.

Now, that same person—who works in the retail business, is the chief executive of a major name in large-scale distribution, and is very familiar with retail sales—claims that my prediction came as a blinding revelation and that he hasn't stopped thinking about it since. I don't believe him (but journalists do love flattery!). I was simply making a straightforward observation, and it wasn't an especially difficult one—for two basic reasons.

First reason. It was obvious that, sooner or later, online shopping would demolish the wall of Italian reluctance—still a robust bulwark—and ford the swamps of home delivery (a logistical challenge). In Italy, we frequently mistake mere challenges to the advent of a new technology for the actual failure of that same technology. How many opinion pieces did I write for *Corriere della Sera* about the challenges of email (in the 1990s)? How many diatribes against the general scarcity of Wi-Fi (in the early 2000s) and our initial distrust in smartphones a few years later?

Second reason. Western society—of which we Italians are members, even if we occasionally forget the fact—is growing lazier at a rapid and progressive pace. Less and less frequently

do we bother to go out and shop, instead we expect our purchases to come to us: movies and TV series (Netflix, Amazon Prime), music (Spotify, YouTube), audiobooks (Audible),
physical books (Amazon), sports (Sky), food (Glovo, Deliv-
eroo), cars (Uber), news (from the *New York Times* to *Corriere
della Sera* to Twitter), and friendships (Facebook, Instagram,
and all the rest). It is obvious that the same will happen with
shopping as soon as payment and delivery systems become
sufficiently rapid, secure, and efficient. At that point, an
implacable mechanism is bound to kick in: brick-and-mortar
stores will start to lose customers and revenue, and they will
start to retrench; our pursuit of a certain product in a physical store will become increasingly chancy and frustrating; the
incentives for e-commerce will proliferate.

Alongside these two reasons, we can add a third: the
requirement of distancing imposed by the pandemic. It's not a
passing consideration, unfortunately: everything points to the
likelihood that we're going to be reckoning with viruses for
some time to come. There are now vaccines against Covid, but
new threats will no doubt pop up. Given these circumstances,
e-commerce will enjoy new opportunities. The web serves as
the shop window and the catalog (displaying products and services) as well as the cash register (to make and receive payments). The delivery itself, however, has not changed, except in
terms of the time frame: slippers ordered on Amazon, from that
point of view, are no different from slippers ordered through
Postal Market, Italy's equivalent of the Sears catalog.

Of course, Amazon is the unquestioned champion in this
new race. It is the world's largest online marketplace, with 1.3
million employees and huge sales worldwide. (Should we ask
Amazon to pay taxes on those sales? It might not be a bad
idea.)

I remember when I went to Seattle in 2000 to interview Jeff Bezos. The big boss himself explained to me what he had in mind for his company. Take profits immediately? That didn't matter. Get big fast; now *that* was the point. Win market share, even if it meant losing money. Service the customer with fanatical zeal. Our competitors are never going to love us, and politicians might, but only when it's useful to them, he said between bursts of laughter. But if our customers are satisfied, they'll never leave us.

Can we call that an obvious conclusion? Perhaps, but it is necessary to understand that certain rules of the analog world will apply just as strictly to the digital world. "The customer is always right," employees in brick-and-mortar stores in the twentieth century used to say. *Customers rule!* Bezos wrote when he signed his biography for me. The transformation is global; what's happened in Italy has happened practically everywhere (in China, the eight-hundred-pound gorilla isn't Amazon—it's Alibaba). And there aren't just tech giants, as we know very well: every company out there, if its product line permits, now accepts orders online and makes home deliveries or ships via regular delivery services. And if it hasn't, it will soon.

And where *hasn't* it happened? In countries where demographics, unreliable payment facilities, the situation of the cities, and the state of the postal service all prevent or make it challenging to place orders and make deliveries. If someday the situation changes there, you can rest assured that e-commerce will quickly bloom there. Young would-be Bezoses are growing up all over, even though we have no idea where they are or what they have in mind.

There's only one thing that can get us to go places and spend money for a service that is anything other than indispensable: an enjoyable experience. That is why bookstores remain places with an unmistakable allure. That is why, as we have seen, the *aperitivo* had become a philosophical category and restaurants were thriving until the lockdown, and they will surely come back in the future, as well, provided that they offer two hours worth remembering, and not just a bite of nutritious food to gulp down.

Another pleasant experience is to avoid a useless chore. Why are corner stores—now renamed proximity stores—so successful? And why have some, in the time of Covid, seemed to experience a second childhood and a new youth? Because corner stores let you forgo travel, parking, lines, and stress. Many—and I saw this in Crema in 2020 and 2021—showed a great sense of civic responsibility and passion in taking on their new role, featuring a greater assortment of products, a more welcoming atmosphere, greater customer service: necessity created the demand, the demand led to better supply, the supply incentivized the owners and managers to double down and invest in offering better service.

There are the little supermarket on Via Verdi; Cornalba butchers, Scandelli delicatessen, the bakers, the vegetable and fruit stands of various nationalities that compete to stock the juiciest oranges; the Play Sport apparel shop with Roberto smiling at the door; the herbal medicine shop, the hardware store, the tobacconists, the bookshops, the Egyptian barber with posters autographed by the soccer star Momo Salah; the optical shop Guarneri Ottica, which still is and always will be for me La Fonte dell'Occhiale—the Source of the Eyeglasses— a name that I find vaguely Petrarchesque; Chizzoli emporium, also known as Il Gomma, on Via Mazzini; the cafés (Bar

Teatro, Bar Bettolino, Bar Marini, Bar Torrefazione, and the others), with their open-air tables and sweet-smelling disinfectant; pharmacies and newsstands. On Piazza del Duomo, Angelo hands you your morning paper, complete with a five-word microeditorial. And when a newspaper publishes nonsense, he hangs up its daily flyer sideways, so if you want to read the headline, it'll cost you a crick in your neck.

Crema is a network of services within reach, a flat, compact city, ideal for getting around on foot or on two wheels. To do what we can accomplish in half an hour, an American has to drive twenty miles and spend half a day. A shop—when the shopkeeper knows what he's doing—is a place for meeting and talking matters through. The barber Gigi on Via Tensini, a tennis player and Milan supporter, charges twenty euros for a haircut and shampoo: inexpensive, given the psychotherapy session that comes with it. The covered market on Via Verdi, with the old stalls and the new social distancing, is not an alternative to the Coop hypermarket on the road to Milan. The customers are the same. You ride to the covered market on your bicycle, you go to the Ipercoop by car; we people of Crema, from a certain age on, know how to get around in either.

During the period of lockdown, all that was a given. The shops near our homes showed that they were capable of competing even against e-commerce in spite of its convenience, its rapidity, and its lower prices. They can continue to do so. It's up to them. But most of all, it's up to us.

42. Because in the restaurant business, people weather the storm with a smile

When we hear thunder in Crema, we look at the sky.

Pegurì, pegurù, sbròfacaai, bröt cantù.

In our dialect, *pegurì* are little sheep: the shape of clouds toward Bergamo, to the north.

Pegurù are big sheep: more robust clouds from Brescia, to the east.

Sbròfacaai means that the storm will be coming from the south, from Cremona—usually not much of a downpour, just a light sprinkle for the horses, as the formers put it in dialect.

Bröt cantù, the nasty corner, is the one to the northwest, toward Milan. Treacherous downbursts come from that direction. In that case, it's time to batten down the hatches.

People look up at the sky, at tiny Lake Sarius between Sergnano and Pianengo, when bad weather is brewing. If the rain comes down heavy and the Serio River rises sharply, real trouble can ensue. It's happened before. During the last instance, on October 30, 2018, the flood hit a high point of one meter. The marks it left are still visible on building walls. This is a place where Mother Nature gives and Mother Nature takes away; it's up to her. The lake is more than twelve acres of clear spring water, carp and pike swimming under the surface, ducks floating on the surface, trees standing all around it: poplars, plane trees, locusts, mulberries, and hazelnut trees. On the shores are elder trees and willows. The little lake peeps out of the greenery, like a glittering jewel.

When my father bought the land with a partner in 1958, the Cascina Asmara, an old farmhouse, stood here. You'd reach the place from Casale Cremasco, cutting through the woods. Every once in a while, when I was a child, my parents would take me there. It was like stepping into a book of fairy tales. A powerfully built man, short and taciturn, lived in the farmhouse. He'd vanish into the poplars on a cart pulled by two horses, which seemed enormous to me.

The land, next to the river, was full of gravel. Gravel of that grade was in great demand in the early 1970s, when many people were interested in building or buying a house. A quarry was authorized, and it resulted in the first spring-fed pond. After the construction of the Melotta provincial road, which runs from Soncino to Spino d'Adda, access became easier. People called it *il laghetto*—the little lake—and it was a popular place to train hunting dogs and to go skeet shooting, rowing, and even water-skiing. The carp under the surface pretended not to notice.

In 1977, a trattoria was opened in the old farmhouse. On the south side, amid the poplars, my uncle Rino gathered his friends in the *tés*, the old hut, camouflaged as a blind for duck hunting, which had become a place to get together, make coffee, and watch the sunset. The water was stocked not only with herbivorous carp but also with chub and largemouth bass; someone tried to start sport fishing there, but the experiment was a failure. Perhaps the fisherman disturbed Tarantasio the Dragon, which according to legend inhabited the ancient Lake Gerundo between the Adda and Serio rivers.

In the 1990s, gravel continued to be quarried, and the little lake grew from five to twelve acres. But for years it remained

fenced off and the environmental restoration—a legal obligation that came with the right to quarry—kept being pushed
off. In the early years of the first decade of the twenty-first
century, the trattoria reopened, with the gravel quarry still
operating. It was a complicated period, with repeated changes
of management. At last, in 2016, we decided to take the management back and my son, Antonio, spoke up. "It's a beautiful
place, and I have an idea," he said.

For two years he fixed things up, swept and scrubbed,
planned, renovated, planted, labored, and reinforced. The
result is twenty-five acres of magnificent greenery. The north-
western part is protected wetlands. There are spontaneous
flora, a large vegetable garden, a fruit orchard, a chicken house;
two dogs, Winston and Alba; two donkeys and two goats;
ducks and hares; crystal-clear water; a small bridge leading
into the marsh, where the fish go to spawn; a wharf with six
rowboats. On the eastern shore, on April 3, 2019, he opened the
bar/restaurant Sarius al Lago. The food is delicious, there's
good wine to wash it down, and it's a happy place.

Antonio and his group—only one of them is older than
thirty—refused to let themselves be discouraged by the flood
(fall 2018), the hurricane (summer 2019), or the pandemic
(2020–2021). When they smell a thunderstorm in the offing, they
look up to the sky. If the black clouds are marching toward
them from the *bröt cantù*, they warn the customers, lower the
awnings and umbrellas, empty the refrigerators, secure the
wine, carry the chickens and dogs to safety, park the tractor
at the highest elevation on the property, and then wait to see
what happens.

In Italian restaurants, people smile, even when it's thunder-
ing and pouring down rain.

43. Because in our parks, we love strolling, relaxing, and quarreling

Every morning, Indro Montanelli, Italy's most influential journalist of the twentieth century, used to go for a walk by himself in the gardens of Porta Venezia in Milan. Tall and skinny, he would nod to his readers while planning his articles and books. Now, amid those trees and lawns, there is a bronze statue of him. He's sitting on a stack of newspapers, his typewriter on his knees. Signor Montanelli wouldn't have approved. He despised statues and monuments. "They're only good for pigeons, because they poop on them," he used to say.

There are people who want to expel him from the park. May I express my opinion? Those people are wrong.

I don't say it because Indro Montanelli is an immense source of pride for Milan, the city he loved and for which he literally shed blood (the Red Brigades shot him in 1977; afterward he forgave his attackers). I don't say it because he was a glorious veteran of *Corriere della Sera*, to which he returned in 1995, after founding *Il Giornale* and editing it for twenty years and also after venturing into the short-lived enterprise of *La Voce*. I don't say it because he taught so many of us our profession—and supported us.

I say it because as a man and as a journalist, he doesn't deserve an affront of the sort; nor does Milan, Italy, or the Italians. Overturning the statue of a dictator may be an act of liberation; overturning the statue of a free and decent journalist smacks of fanaticism.

The story in question dates back to 1935. Indro Montanelli—

a somewhat world-weary, cocky young Fascist reporter—left for the African front. He had just turned twenty-six. Once he reached Asmara, he was mustered in as a company commander in the Twentieth Eritrean Battalion, made up of local mercenaries known as Ascari, a ragtag, inefficient unit, largely assigned to behind-the-lines duty. Second Lieutenant Montanelli wrote, "Before us we have an enemy who does nothing but retreat and a local population who do nothing but cheer us on. It's a walk in the park, though not an entirely comfortable one." That adventure is recounted in a book, *XX Battaglione eritreo* (*Twentieth Eritrean Battalion*), which was reviewed favorably in *Corriere della Sera*.

Once in Africa, the young second lieutenant took an Abyssinian adolescent as his girlfriend in accordance with the colonial custom of the *madamato*, which was encouraged by the Italian military command. The girl was named Destà. "Throughout the war, like all the wives of my Ascari men, she managed to make her way to me every fifteen or twenty days, no matter where I'd happened to fetch up in that land without roads or maps." Montanelli, like so many other members of his generation, failed to grasp the profound injustice of that relationship, but he never denied it, nor did he try to erase it from his biography. What we know about the story, we know from his own account of it. We also know that the terribly young Destà was then married to Montanelli's Eritrean attendant, and the couple had three children: they named their firstborn son Indro.

Taking a teenager as a lover—that is deeply wrong, indisputably. Should we remove Montanelli's statue because of it? He certainly made that mistake in his youth, but it doesn't represent the man in his entirety: the journalist, the writer, the beliefs for which he fought. Montanelli ridiculed fascism as a reporter in the Spanish Civil War, and he was punshied for it; he was held prisoner by the Nazis, he fought communism (the real kind), he took a stand against terrorism (and was shot in the legs not far from his monument), he battled for the independence of journalism (against Berlusconi among others), he refused political accolades, and he educated two generations of Italian moderates. None of that counts, however, in the eyes of certain critics. If an isolated episode were enough to disqualify a life, not a single statue would remain standing, except for statues of the saints, and not even all of those.

Last of all: doubling down in a crusade against the figure of Indro Montanelli would be counterproductive. If the city government of Milan did agree to remove his statue—out of meek conformism and lazy indifference—it would deliver the gift of many moderates to the worst kind of right-wing extremists, who would welcome them with open arms. It's happened elsewhere, for instance, in the United States: intolerant progressives generated a general irritation among moderates that helped send Donald Trump to the White House.

So let's leave the statue where it now stands in the Giardini Montanelli. It helps us to think.

44. Because we've elevated complaining to an art form

Eternally he flatters
Eternally he chatters
Eternally licks platters
And pretends he's so sad.

A slim gray volume calls out from the highest shelf and offers this epigram. The title of the collection is *Quiproquo* (1974). The author was Tito Balestra, whose surname meant "crossbow," and he was farsighted and ahead of his time. Those four short lines foretell a type of human that's especially successful these days in Italy.

Before saying more about that human category, a word or two about the poet. Born in 1923 in Longiano, a small town in Romagna—a region of great artistic vitality—Balestra moved to Rome in 1946 to study to become a social worker. He lived with his aunt and uncle: he was a bricklayer, and she was a *portinaia*, a sort of concierge, in an apartment building. "He arrived at art from the lowliest apprenticeship," to use his own words. He spent his time frequenting art galleries and newsrooms. He got to know prominent figures in the arts, including Corrado Alvaro, Giorgio Bassani, Attilio Bertolucci, Ennio Flaiano, Renato Guttuso, Mino Maccari, and Leo Longanesi, a fellow *romagnolo*. And he wrote. Alfonso Gatto had this to say about him: "Balestra is a poet who was in no hurry to print his work, a poet who only his friends even knew wrote poetry."

Little could Balestra have dreamed that one of his poems, nearly half a century later, would so effectively describe a national protagonist: the man who is unhappy by profession. This human type never stands up and protests, but he complains. He doesn't state, he contradicts. He doesn't criticize, he deplores. He's the kind of Italian who invariably feels that everything is a disaster. And nothing, of course, is ever his fault.

Fair enough. It's heartbreaking to observe the way that the coronavirus has further hobbled an economy that was already limping. It's no fun to look at your paycheck and find that instead of fattening, it has shrunk. It's not great to have your children staying home from school or see them casting about for a job. It's not comforting to see someone who already did as little as possible take advantage of the crisis to do even less. It's not a pretty sight to behold politicians down in the courtyard like so many birds of prey, ready to peck at whatever they find lying around. But the apocalypse—can we agree?—is quite another matter.

To be worried in today's Italy is normal. But to despair is offensive to those who have lived through true horrors or still are doing so (war, say, terrorism, or political or religious persecution). Or to someone who has a family and is suffering the genuine anguish of not knowing how to pay for groceries and bills. Someone who is unhappy by profession, however, will have none of this. He lives inside his own pocket-sized nightmare, and he wants the world to know it.

Let's say it again: there is no shortage of reasons for dismay in Italy: decision makers who can't seem to decide, directors who have no sense of direction, industrialists who dabble in high finance instead of manufacturing, a sector of the political class that seeks out and nurtures discontent, and social networks and mass media that too often merely fan the flames. None of that, however, justifies a perpetual lament—because the Italians possess a rich array of resources that we have tried to lay out in this book; and because complaining does no good.

The jeremiad may have become, perhaps, a new form of artistic expression. But it remains an exhausting, pointless, repetitive kind of activity, a type of social onanism that produces nothing, except for new complaints and renewed exhaustion in those who are forced to listen.

45. Because we love to baffle those who judge us

Members of the League Party become Fascists. Progressives become Communists. Liberals are dismissed as mere radical chic. And it's not happening just in Italy. American Democrats, for example, are often demonized by Republicans as socialists. That's not exactly an obscenity, but in the United States it's certainly tantamount to a disqualification. It's a war of labels, and it promises nothing good.

Labels have appealed to politicians of all persuasions throughout history and in every country: a label is a form of concise, succinct marketing, one that's unfailingly effective in political rallies and is even now useful on social media and TV talk shows. Labels don't provide food for thought; they tend to gag a speaker and to silence a conversation. Benito Mussolini was a tireless fountainhead of labels; they didn't always correspond to reality, but they did help to reinforce his promises and to add color to his threats. The fabled expression "perfidious Albion" wasn't even original to him. But, as a way to mortify England and the English, it still seems to come in handy every now and then.

Populist, chauvinist, and *jingoist* are likewise labels. Have they helped us to think clearly about what's going on in the world? It doesn't seem so. They lump together situations, ideas, and people that are far too ill sorted. Does *nationalist* really serve as a common denominator linking the czar's successor (Vladimir Putin of Russia), the latter-day emperor (Xi Jinping of China), the egocentric tycoon (Donald Trump of the United

States), the histrionic prime minister (Boris Johnson of Great Britain), and the centralizing autocrat (Viktor Orbán of Hungary)? I rather doubt it. Once certain terminology is introduced, any discussion becomes an uphill battle.

Yet labels are stuck onto more or less everything. They're even plastered over our eyes, blinding us. After all, that is exactly what this new breed of politics is all about: the discouragement of rational thought and its replacement with feelings: anxiety, fear, distaste, anger, relief, euphoria, and even hope (though that last one seems to have gone out of fashion). For democracy, this is a dangerous undertow. Because these feelings can be monitored on the internet and by means of artificial intelligence, they can be shaped and harnessed to sway a general election.

In Italy, it is important for us to learn to read these political labels just as we might the label on a bottle of olive oil. The problem is that in politics, you're not going to find much that's extra-virgin.

꿈

I have found myself, when outside Italy, explaining Italian characters whom I criticize when in Italy—not out of love of country but rather love of precision. For twenty years I found myself forced to explain to Americans and Brits that we deserved better than Silvio Berlusconi. Then, for five years, I tried to persuade them that Berlusconi, in comparison with Trump, is Winston Churchill.

Certainly, Silvio and Donald do have their family resemblances: they're both businessmen who like to play it fast and loose and who tend primarily to their own self-interest; they're both charismatic, persuasive, and vain; and each has a complicated and tormented relationship with his ego and his head of hair. They both have harassed women far too young for them. But the similarities stop there. Berlusconi was a moderate head of government, he believed in NATO and the European Union, and he wanted to be loved by all Italians. Trump is an impulsive extremist, and he worked tirelessly to divide the nation when he should have been uniting it.

Then it was Matteo Salvini's turn. Many of my foreign colleagues had no real interest in understanding who he was or what he was planning. All they wanted from me was confirmation that Salvini was a Fascist. I tried to explain: Matteo Salvini sometimes pets and grooms the Fascists, which is a problem. Certain dubious statements of his are insidious; his Mussolini-esque use of balconies is perilous. But Salvini is no Fascist. He's a wily populist, ready and willing to say anything, or the exact opposite, if it helps him to poll better. He'll take up a machine gun, gulp down cherries during a dramatic press conference, wave a rosary, insult or praise the European Union, and deliver a political stump speech surrounded by dancers in Brazilian thongs on the beach—consistency isn't his strong suit. But we should recognize one positive trait of the League and its leader: they've never practiced or threatened violence.

The same goes for the Five Star Movement. For years, until its victory in the elections of 2018, the verbal aggressivity of the party's voters (and some of its candidates) was hard to take. But actual physical brawls, beatings, or attacks? They never happened. There are even those who defend Beppe Grillo's obscenities, saying that the systematic insults he spouts serve as a sort of safety valve. On social media, horrifying comments have appeared along with nauseatingly offensive attacks. But getting in touch with the offending commenters helps one to sufficiently realize that, most of the time, they aren't the savage monsters they want to be taken for—they're just weak, pathetic individuals. When I edited *Corriere della Sera*'s weekly magazine 7, we discovered that the target of a criminal complaint for appalling insults against the speaker of the Italian Parliament was a young man who slept with a teddy bear, whatever that meant.

The absence of political violence is something we Italians should take credit for. It's a point of pride we should vaunt in Europe and around the world. To those who look down their noses at our democracy, we might well point out that in Italy, our capital hasn't been besieged by organized violent mobs for months on end, as has been the case in France; that disagreements about regional independence haven't resulted in clashes and arrests, as was the case in Spain; that our social existence isn't constantly blighted by massacres and mass shootings the way it is in the United States. Our disgust with violence is unmistakable when it comes time to cast votes, as well: extremist brawlers—and we do have a few—win only tiny percentages.

Great international concern greeted the formation of a national coalition government composed of the Five Star Movement and the League in 2018, with an unknown and untested law professor, Giuseppe Conte, as prime minister. Matteo Salvini, deputy prime minister and minister of the interior, missed no opportunity to praise Vladimir Putin and Russia and spoke freely of exiting the euro. The leaders of the Five Star Movement were thrilled with Donald Trump, acclaimed the Venezuelan strongman Nicolás Maduro, and mocked and derided the European Union; Prime Minister Conte held his tongue. Nearly all the media of Europe and the United States were convinced that the first populist government of the West would drag Italy straight into the abyss and that Italy would drag the rest of Europe down with it.

I've explained, every time I've had the chance, that there's an operatic aspect to Italian political life. How many times can the soprano threaten to throw herself off the tower or to stab herself in the chest? She seldom does if she's not Tosca. The Italians quarrel in spectacular fashion (in Parliament, on television, at the Sanremo Music Festival, in cafés, in homes, wherever they get the itch), but when it comes time to make real decisions, most display surprising caution. We know Europe is our home. We know our allies are in Brussels, London, and Washington, DC—not in Moscow. We know violence is revolting and leads nowhere good, because we've experienced it.

The coalition government established by the League and the Five Star Movement lasted fourteen months and achieved only modest results, but it didn't drag Italy into the abyss. Then emerged an alliance of two former adversaries, the Five Star Movement and the Democratic Party, with the same prime minister, Giuseppe Conte, suddenly cheerful and chipper. He changed from a silent populist to a loquacious guarantor of the established institutions. The new government faced the terrible ordeal of the pandemic, a challenge that it overcame. It mended Italy's tattered relationship with the European Union. The vagueness that ensued—and that led to a national unity government in 2021—cannot erase those achievements.

Foreign observers look at all this and, unsurprisingly, are confused. Let's try to be understanding of their bafflement. Let's just say to them: Italy is a difficult exam. We often flunk it ourselves.

46. Because we know that sometimes those who judge us are right

Between the tongue and the hands, in Italy, the distance is too great. Between what we say and what we do there often passes too much time, and too many permits are required, too many arguments ensue, too much consultation drags out, and too many doubts are entertained. Too many people are afraid of taking responsibility; they postpone, slow walk, and delay. This is a general condition we've grown accustomed to, though we pay a high price. But then the pandemic unexpectedly changed everything. Uncertainty is a luxury we can no longer afford.

Europe is studying us, the United States is watching us; we need to live up to this moment. The projects of the National Recovery and Resilience Plan call for outlays of more than two hundred billion euros; basically, it's a new Marshall Plan, this time financed by the European Union. Digitalization and innovation; green revolution and ecological transition; new infrastructure for sustainable mobility; funds for education and research; labor policies, social inclusion, aid to families with children, and a reduction of the gap between North and South; health care.

The relief that other governments, institutions, and international organizations and markets displayed when Mario Draghi took charge of a new administration is comforting for Italy. But that relief is directly proportional to their astonishment and concern. Mario Draghi—a former president of the European Central Bank, the rescuer of the euro in 2012—is probably the most respected Italian on Earth right now. His reputation is that of an authoritative and sensible man, one capable of planning and allergic to empty promises and cheap sentimentalism. He is a seal of confidence, but he's also the best guarantee we can offer.

What's at stake is our reputation. Beyond our national borders, there is more than just other governments, institutions, organizations, and markets; there is also a global public opinion that, when times are normal, can often be fickle and shallow. In this convulsive beginning to the 2020s, it can be brutal. Every other country in the world is facing its own challenges: economic, political, social, psychological, and health care problems. None of them has time for our problems.

So let's try to be honest with ourselves. There exists a risk that Italy may be treated like a goofy piece of folklore. It's not an exaggeration, I'm afraid.

Over the long months of obligatory distancing and travel prohibitions, I've read, listened, watched, thought, and weighed matters carefully. As a writer, I've delivered lectures and held webinars. As a journalist, I've taken part in seminars, meetings, debates, and conversations online: with the European Commission in Brussels; with associations and universities in the United States, from California to Virginia; with directors of multinational corporations with strong ties to Italy; with politicians, ex-politicians, and future politicians; with American, Canadian, Brazilian, British, French, Polish, Spanish, Indian, and Chinese colleagues and acquaintances—a diverse array of people, topics, and times with only one constant, one through line: "Ah, you Italians! Your governments may change, but you're still the same." There were times when they said it to my face with varying nuances of sympathy. Other times they just let it show.

What should I reply? That the current Italian government—the sixty-seventh government in eighteen legislatures spanning seventy-five years (with an average life span of thirteen and a half months)—is sure to be exceptionally stable? That it will do everything that our friends and allies expect it to?

Italy is a central load-bearing architrave of the European Union, an institution it helped found in the 1950s. If Italy were to fail, the European edifice would collapse. Italy is too heavy to be held up if it falls; and too important for anyone to think it can simply be allowed to tumble. Former German chancellor Angela Merkel understood that clearly during her final stretch of time in office: for Germany, Italy represents a huge market, a magnificent vacation (both physical and psychological), an example (for better or worse), a reminder, and an examination of conscience. We'll never be a matter of indifference to those who live across the Alps.

When it comes to Italians—there is no point concealing the fact—there is always a systemic suspicion of unreliability. It has subsided in recent years, thanks to our many invaluable compatriots around the world. And it has further waned over the course of the pandemic, during which the Italians—as described in the first portion of this book—acquitted themselves with distinction, displaying courage, resilience, and patience (at times quite a bit was required). Italians of all ages, of all extractions, from every walk of life and every range of opinion have accepted sacrifice, both personal and family.

This is capital we can't afford to squander.

Mario Draghi, who has been traveling the world for fifty years, knows this: national stereotypes are superficial and frequently ferocious. But they exist, and they condition the attitudes of international institutions, other nations, markets, and overhasty global public opinion. The world at large—I'm sure my non-Italian readers will agree—has no time nor interest in delving into the details of our political affairs. It just wants to know if we're serious and if they can rely on us.

Often those who judge us are annoying, it's true. But occasionally they are right.

47. Because if nobody's the same, it's hard to feel different

A man in his early seventies, with a garish printed shirt and a tangle of fierce black hair, stops me on the piazza. He introduces himself and explains what a hard life he has led. He's worked milking cows since he was just a boy, and he's only recently retired. He tells me, "I listen to you all the time on TV. You're too soft on immigrants.

"I want them out of Italy," he adds.

"All of them?" I ask.

"All of them. I don't want a single one left here."

"Then who'll take care of me and you in a few years?" I ask. "Caregivers and nurses in Italy are nearly all foreigners: they come from Eastern Europe, South America, Sri Lanka, and the Philippines."

"Italians will do it," he replies.

"I have my doubts," I tell him. "Italians aren't interested in certain lines of work. They don't even want your old job. Milkers in the Italian countryside, as you know, generally come from India. Farmhands and field-workers in southern Italy come from Africa. You find lots of Romanians and Albanians working on scaffoldings on construction sites. In our cafés and restaurants, you'll find Chinese, Egyptians, and Tunisians. Are you really sure you want to get rid of them all? Italy would grind to a halt almost instantly, like a car out of gas."

The man with the garish shirt mutters something, tells me goodbye, and leaves.

⁓⊱⊰⁓

I found this photograph on Facebook or maybe Instagram, I can't remember. It made an impression on me. I have a great love of Sardinia, as I've said; it's a place I know well. That little girl, dark skinned and in a traditional outfit, was striking, unusual, and lovely. I thought to myself: *What a nice picture. That family understands an important thing: you need to love the land that takes you in, accept its customs and ways.* That's the only path to integration, a way of building a peaceable coexistence.

Then I heard about the comments. The musician Claudia Aru—who had shared the photograph, taken and posted by a young man from Tortolì, Cristopher Porcu—was appalled: comments that called for and condoned extermination, advocacy of death, and a witch's brew of assorted racist filth.

I'll confess, I wouldn't willingly have included this story as a concluding piece to a book that I'd like to think offers a bounty of hope; certain types of people don't need extra publicity. What convinced me to talk about it here was the reaction of Sardinians at large: honest, affectionate, and immediate. These are the Italians I know and love: people who demand respect but offer it in return; people who welcome their fellow human beings with open arms, well aware that it's the right and farsighted thing to do.

Claudia Aru recalled, "Hundreds of people wrote me. Many illustrators created fantastic drawings, taking that photograph as inspiration, sharing them online." This isn't naive idealism, it isn't sentimentalism, it isn't just Christian charity (something many Christians seem to have forgotten about: Has it gone out of fashion?). It's just good common sense. And a sound investment. Those children of different ethnic groups are not just Italy's future, they're our present; you can see it if you open your eyes, if you visit any school. Do you remember the school bus that was hijacked with fifty-one students aboard and then set afire on March 20, 2019? It was coming from the Giovanni Vailati middle school in Crema, an educational institution my son, my wife, and my father all attended. The fanatic driving the bus was born in Africa, but read the story of the two youngsters who secretly managed to phone the carabinieri, bringing the hijacking to a safe resolution. Their families came from Africa, too, from Morocco. Now they've both become Italian citizens.

The Italian population of foreign origin is now about 8 percent—within the average range for the European Union—and it's largely concentrated in the north of the country. Half come from elsewhere in Europe, a quarter from Romania alone. The immigrants who landed in Italy in 2017 were 118,914 in number; in 2018, 23,210; in 2019, 11,439; and in the first half of 2020, 6,812. These aren't numbers that ought to frighten a major European democracy, one of the world's seven top economic powerhouses.

There's another complicated issue. The undocumented immigrants present in Italy, according to estimates, are roughly six hundred thousand in number: one out of every hundred people on Italian soil. Among them are not only immigrants who've been denied asylum or protection but foreigners with expired tourist visas and those who no longer have a residency permit. In the face of this situation, there are three possible paths forward: track them all down and expel them from the country (but how?); methodically bring them into compliance; or allow them to become ghost residents. But desperate ghosts are unpredictable. Is that a risk we're eager to run?

The vast majority of Italians aren't ranting and objecting. Many of those who rant and object to foreigners are merely frightened and confused. Immigration simply hasn't been explained or managed particularly well in Italy. Refusing Italian citizenship to children born and raised in Italy by foreign parents is wrong. Leaving so many young Africans out on the streets has been a colossal misstep: for Italians who were already struggling to make ends meet every month, it seemed like a slap in the face, a provocation, and petty crime just found a new source of manpower, easy to recruit and exploit. That said, let's be careful: certain slogans are dangerous, certain attitudes are disastrous. Either the future of Italy is multiethnic or it isn't. Our demographics, our history, and our geography all say that it is. And so does that photograph.

Anyone who talks about a "pure Italian race" is raving. The mere concept of "human race" is devoid of any scientific basis. The geneticist Alberto Piazza, who worked at Stanford University with Luigi Luca Cavalli-Sforza, has explained the "incredible heterogeneity" of the Italians, so much so that there are genetic differences between bordering regions of Italy that are comparable to, say, those found between a Spaniard and a Dane. "A mosaic of clearly differentiated ethnic groups"—that is how Professor Piazza describes Italy. "The result of the many migrations that have passed through our country since ancient times."

We're a beautiful blend, the product of different places, the result of time, love, and random chance. How can anyone feel different in Italy, if nobody's the same?

48. Because occasionally we're speechless, but eventually we find the words

The 2010s were a complicated decade for Italy, a challenging trek with three great uphill climbs.

The first uphill climb: The global financial crisis of 2009 was absorbed slowly and asymmetrically. Italy has shown the slowest growth of any economy in Europe over the past ten years. Since we scraped bottom during the second quarter of 2013, our gross domestic product has increased by 4 percent: a trifle, less than half the growth in Greece, Portugal, and Finland, the next above us at the bottom of the ranking. In the face of various challenges to development, an implacable tax burden, and a costly and suffocating regulatory regime, companies have tried to cut where they could: on salaries. In Italy, today, salaries are lower than the European average. Not even an open-ended employment contract necessarily means that you'll be able to afford to own a home, raise a family, and enjoy a decent standard of living anymore.

The second uphill climb: the 2010s gave the newly impoverished middle class the tools with which to express their discontentment. Unquestionably, the smartphone was the device of the decade. Facebook, Twitter, Instagram, and WhatsApp all established themselves in that period. They have made it possible for anyone to read the news, obtain information, and express opinions all day long and everywhere. Admittedly, that information and news has frequently been shallow and superficial (and in some cases deliberately false), while the opinions expressed have been, as often as not, reckless or divisive. But for the first time, people have been able to express their opinions without any physical effort or commitment (such as that required on the street or in a protest march). And in Italy we took advantage of that opportunity. Oh, how we took advantage of it!

The third uphill climb: Certain populist movements have proved adept at harvesting and harnessing the unrest. Where the middle class has held out most successfully (France and Germany), those movements have encountered greater resistance; where the middle class has declined most dramatically—in Italy, Great Britain, and the United States—those movements have done land-office business. The election results in the second half of the decade provide a clear picture. The frustration of the American middle class elected Donald Trump. The overweening nostalgia of the British middle class led it to opt for Brexit and vote Boris Johnson into power. The bitter disappointment of the Italian middle class found expression in votes for the Five Star Movement and the League.

If this was what the 2010s were like, what should we expect in the 2020s in the wake of a pandemic that has sown panic and jolted the economy?

The answer is obvious: if discontent continues to swell, the demagogues will have a field day. They'll continue to offer an outlet for popular frustration; they'll go on proposing simple solutions to complex problems. What does it matter if health care, the environment, trade, migration, data protection, and terrorism are global questions? The soapbox speakers of the day will shout that these issues can be easily solved right here at home, and they will find willing listeners. Only after time passes will the con game become evident. And a demagogue unmasked can turn dangerous.

What should we hope for? First off, that reasonable people

will display courage. Being moderate isn't enough. Those who believe in progress, cooperation, and an open society must make their voices heard. They will have to dare greatly. The panicky management of the proliferation of brush fires is no longer sufficient. In fact, it never has been.

Being moderate doesn't mean being pusillanimous; it means being farsighted. The social achievements we can rightly be proud of—our national health service, our public education system, a justice system independent of political power—came about in the West only after great and devastating traumas: dictatorships and wars. Today, too, there are important tasks to be completed in Italy. Our schools, our health care system, our public administration, and our system of justice all need to be modernized, simplified, and streamlined. Our tax system is a threadbare fabric that has been mended, darned, and patched for decades; it needs to be replaced entirely. Our road network and railways need to be modernized. The Italian national territory is a fragile creation; we can't put off action any longer.

Let's not wait for the cataclysm before speaking up. Occasionally, we're speechless. But eventually we will find the words.

49. Because we are what others would love to be, but don't dare

Beauty isn't a privilege. Beauty isn't a facade. Beauty isn't a mitigating factor. Italian beauty is a responsibility.

It's a simple concept, and the world understands it clearly. But Italy and we Italians seem to have a harder time grasping it. Frequently, those who speak of beauty are just trying to cover a series of eyesores: in the landscape, in our planning, in our upkeep, and in our management. Too many Italians justify the pettiness of their behavior with the magnificence of their ambitions—a hypocrisy that has cost us dearly in terms of reputation.

International public opinion isn't especially sophisticated. If we say, "Italy may not function as efficiently as we'd like, but it sure is pretty!" we can expect a round of applause from some quarters. That applause, however, absolves and distracts; it doesn't help. Beauty, like any other significant inheritance, demands effort. The spectacular variety that Italy offers in terms of people, climate, landscape, art, and food cannot simply be a constant refrain on the lips of resigned citizens or a handy excuse for cunning administrators and incompetent politicians. Beauty is mute; it can't defend itself when it's insulted. We are the ones who must take action.

It's no accident that the Italian film best known around the world in the past several years is titled *La grande bellezza* (*The Great Beauty*). Nor should it come as a surprise that it's been especially popular with non-Italians, to the point that it won an Oscar in 2014. Paolo Sorrentino proved that he's not only a fine director but also a capable marketing manager. Rome is recounted by Jep Gambardella, a society journalist specializing in cynicism, conversation, and all-nighters. It's a heartbreaking city, as diseased as it is beautiful. Organized crime, Vatican scandals, a checkered history of collusion and corruption, the ineffectual efforts of a string of mayors, the inefficacy of city services, all of it decked out in great beauty— which simply wasn't enough.

"With his mischievous pout, the main character suggests a Roman-style Walter Matthau, as he contemplates the glories of the only city on earth capable of making him feel the scope of eternity," wrote the critic at the French daily *Le Monde.* "A swooning love letter to Roman decadence," commented Britain's *Guardian.* "The Glory of Rome, the Sweetness of Life" was the headline of the *New York Times* review. Our domestic critics were more unforgiving; Italian audiences, less enthusiastic. Why?

La grande bellezza is less persuasive to Italians because it worries them, and it wins more favor with foreigners because it heartens them. It is a paradoxical but effective account of a city capable of digesting anything: popes, governments, pilgrims, tourists, artistic genius, high-society ambitions, literary fantasies, magnificent bodies, techno music, sacred music. Rome hardly represents all of Italy, but it does exemplify its history, its grandeur, and its pitfalls. Beauty, in a word. Beauty and its consequences.

Jep Gambardella, played by Toni Servillo, is a paradoxical character. But he becomes the efficacious eyewitness of a place and a nation that conceal their anxieties behind an apparent carefree brio. The film's characters are like the statues along the Pincio Promenade: they're there to remind us that in Italy and Rome practically everything imaginable has happened, but it might all just as well be nothing. It is this sensation, vast and sweeping but at the same time anguish laden, that so many Italians disliked—because it reminded us that the great beauty may also turn out to be a great and unbearable ballast: it intimidates and consoles, repeats and reassures, enfeebles and hinders.

We have proved our ability to narrate, sing, act, paint, sculpt, and clothe life as no one else in the history of the world. It's magnificent. But it's not enough.

Esthetic pleasure dominates Italian public life, from the provincial piazza to the *palazzi* of the powerful. The passion for maintaining an unrivaled appearance—*la bella figura*, an expression that really defies translation—is the key to understanding our national character. It drives us to dress well, furnish and decorate tastefully, travel with style. It helps us recognize both the elegance of a suit and the harmony of a painting. It pushes us to perform generous, poetic, even theatrical gestures. But, as we have explained, it often prevents us from translating fine gestures into good behavior.

La grande bellezza won favor outside Italy because it demonstrated that behind every Italian weakness there lurks a fine quality and vice versa; because its characters, so anxious and mercurial, are universal. Italy, to the eyes of the world, is a playground of feelings, a concentrate of sensuality and possibility. Foreigners perceive it, even from afar. They're attracted to us, and they mistrust us; they admire us, and they fear us.

Our great beauty is a great temptation. We Italians are what others would like to be, at least from time to time. But they don't dare.

50. Because we smile, in spite of everything

And let's face it: that's not always easy.

In this witty and entertaining collection of travel tales, acclaimed journalist

BEPPE SEVERGNINI

explores his obsession with trains— and what his rail journeys have taught him about culture and identity.

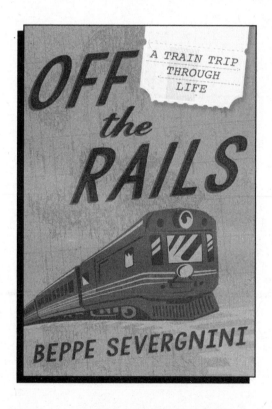

AVAILABLE WHEREVER BOOKS ARE SOLD

ALSO AVAILABLE FROM *NEW YORK TIMES*
BESTSELLING AUTHOR

BEPPE SEVERGNINI

La Bella Figura:
A Field Guide to the Italian Mind

Ciao, America!:
An Italian Discovers the U.S.

"Severgnini is a master."
—PUBLISHERS WEEKLY

CROWN
NEW YORK

Available wherever books are sold